The PORCH SWING COOKBOOK

LETTERS, SONGS AND RECIPES FROM GRANDMOTHER

Web site - Go to Blog. Home (upper left side)
jeanneannecraig.com

JEANNE ANNE CRAIG & SUE EARNEST

outskirts press

Outskirts Press, Inc.
http://www.outskirtspress.com

ISBN: 978-1-9772-1407-2

Library of Congress Control Number: 2019912629

Cover Photo © 2020 www.gettyimages.com. All rights reserved - used with permission.

Outskirts Press and the "OP" logo are trademarks belonging to Outskirts Press, Inc.

PRINTED IN THE UNITED STATES OF AMERICA

We dedicate this book with love to our progeny

*Keri Jo, Craig, Nikki, Lance, Kat, Pamela, Oliver, Zach,
Josh, Tyler, Ian, Devon, Jarris, and Parker*

Sherry, Kelsey, Terence, Funda, Bob, Leonard and Ferdinand

Let's go to bed,

Said Sleepyhead

Let's stay awhile,

Said Slow.

Let's put on the pan,

Said Hungry Nan,

We'll eat before we go.

Anonymous

This is a poem we'd hear our Grandmother say from time to time as she cooked.

TABLE OF CONTENTS

FOREWORD

For a brief period during our early teen years, our grandparents owned a cottage on Sylvan Lake in Rome City, Indiana. It was a magical place—old and musty with a little wood burning stove for heat and cooking and a privy in the backyard. We pumped water in the kitchen and bathed in the lake. There was a screened-in porch in front that overlooked the narrows part of the lake where the cottage was situated. It was furnished with the cast-off furniture from previous owners and featured an old-fashioned porch swing hung from rusty chains.

Often, in the evening after supper or on rainy days that kept us inside, Grandmother would sit in that old porch swing with us snuggled up beside her. We'd slowly and silently rock back and forth to the tune of those creaky chains, sometimes just watching the silvery water as it lapped against the pier. But what we loved best was when Grandmother told stories of her childhood or sang to us sad old songs that had us in gales of laughter—"In the Baggage Coach Ahead" (where the dead mother lay in her coffin), "The Pardon Came Too Late," "Please Don't Give My Daddy No More Wine." We would scream and laugh at the maudlin lyrics while she pretended to be horrified that we were so hard-hearted.

She would also quote the poetry of James Whitcomb Riley, the "Hoosier Poet," or "The Jabberwock," from "Through the Looking

Glass," and other assorted favorites, for she was an inveterate reader. Time seemed endless. Surely it was going to go on forever.

And she cooked. Oh my, did she cook. Both of us have a memory picture of her balancing a finished pie on the tips of her fingers, twisting it around while she trimmed excess pie dough with a table knife in the other hand. She did love to cook, which is strange because she was a mostly indifferent eater herself. But she loved to feed people.

In the years after Sylvan Lake, when we were both married and living in California we carried on a lively correspondence. Her letters were warm and funny and often as not, contained a recipe. We think she was worried that, not having family nearby we'd never learn to cook, and our families would starve. She sent those recipes along with a large measure of love. We offer them to you in the same spirit.

INTRODUCTION

We were born when our parents were much too young to have us. Jeanne Anne was born when our mother was 16 and Sue when she was 18, so like the kids of many teenage parents, we spent a great deal of time with our grandparents—our mother's parents. What a gift!

Granddaddy, as we called him, seldom talked much. We absolutely never heard him raise his voice, though he could sometimes be heard to mutter, "Don't gallop, don't gallop," as we capered joyously through the house. We actually don't know a whole lot about him. He did tell us once that as a young man he had delivered mail on horseback. We decided that meant he was in the Pony Express.

However, it was our grandmother who was the heart of the family. The youngest of a large family, she was doted on by her parents and her much older siblings. And she, in turn was devoted to them. And when we came along a bit earlier than expected, she was equally devoted to us and always let us know it. We adored her.

She lived in Alexandria, Indiana and loved it there. She was known to say that if you were a Presbyterian and a Democrat, you'd surely go to heaven when you died, but that if you lived in Alexandria you wouldn't have to go, for you were already there.

We lived with them off and on for a few years until we started to school. Our father found work after the war in Gas City, about twenty miles from Alec, as it was called, so we moved there where we stayed until high school graduation. But in our memory, every Sunday without fail, the four of us and our dog Peppy would pile into the car and drive to Grandmother's where we made ourselves at home, Sue foraging in the 'Desk' for treasures and Jeanne Anne at the piano while the feast was being assembled. And what a feast it always was!

After high school, Sue married and moved to Los Angeles, with Jeanne Anne and our lifelong friend Patty following not long after. This was in the days before cheap long distance and email, so we wrote letters. And although both of us moved house many times, we managed to save most of hers. It is the content of these letters and the recipes that accompanied them that make up the heart of this book. They were written from about 1960 to 1969. During this time, she experienced the loss of her husband, numerous illnesses, poor housing, never enough money and the vagaries of aging. What was notable, however, was that she did it with grace, courage, good humor and enormous love. It is this recipe for living that we would like to share with you.

FORMAT

As you will see, the true author of this book is our Grandmother, Mary G. Jolliff. We are merely editors. We debated on the format of the book. It made some sense to assemble the letters chronologically, but in the end, we decided to put it together cookbook style with sections for various dishes. Grandmother (she was always called that, never Grandma) usually didn't measure when she cooked, so we've had to translate her amounts into standard measures.

These days, most of the recipes we see are stripped of fat and sugar or are meant to help you get in and out of the kitchen as fast as possible. We think that a Sunday meal, cooked the old-fashioned way with kids hanging around the kitchen "helping," establishes something that goes far beyond the food that will eventually be eaten. So, we've left in all of Grandmother's ingredients. As you will see, it certainly never made her fat. And it embedded in us a precious memory of what families are supposed to be like.

Because she often mentioned the family and friends that surrounded her, we have included a Cast of Characters at the end for the curious. In addition, we have included a glossary of terms, both Grandmother's terms and cooking terms. We included the former because she often used words and phrases not common to all. For example, unlike some mothers and grandmothers of the place and time, she never said, "You kids git in here and warsh them hands fer supper." She said, instead, "You children come and perform your ablutions before you eat."

And for your reading pleasure, we've included an appendix with the lyrics to the porch swing songs and some of the poems, including one she wrote herself. She was the poet laureate of the Rebekah Lodge, but this is the only poem that remains of her prodigious output.

Enjoy!

Jeanne Anne Craig and Sue Earnest
July 2019

The following is a letter Grandmother sent to Jeanne Anne who had gone with her children to Australia to join her husband, who was working there. The people who may need some explaining are our mother, who was a hairdresser, our Uncle Bill, who sometimes lived with her and sometimes did odd jobs, and our Uncle Harry, who was a postman. His smart dog Sam needs no explanation,

November 23, 1965

Dearly Beloved,

I am so glad you called the other day. You can have no idea how good it was to hear all your voices. It is just not fair for families to be so far apart. Well at least your sister is here, which maketh my cup nearly full, but it will not runneth over till you come back.

It must be coming on for summer where you are. Here we are having typical November, Indiana weather--nippy and early morning frost. But the leaves have been so lovely until the past couple of weeks that I can forgive the one who makes the weather.

My cousin, Edna called the other day for your mother to do some rescue work. Seems two blond friends had tried to dye their own hair and it turned out a violent purple. They were quite frantic, as the Rebekah Lodge was doing its Induction Ceremony that week and one was Past Noble Grand and the other an incoming officer. I don't know how it turned out, as I haven't seen your mother since then.

When Bill gets off work, I'm going out to the laundromat to wash my dirty linen, more or less in public. Thanks so much for the stockings you sent me. I was just about out of mates. I have on two perfectly good ones today, but they are many shades from matching, so my legs are totally different colors.

Here is a good way to fix chicken: Take a cut-up fryer (2-3 pounds) Dip the chicken pieces in melted oleo or butter if you're feeling flush—about a half a cube. Salt and pepper to taste. Pulverize two cups of Rice Krispies and roll the chicken in them. Place on a cookie sheet and bake in a 350 oven 30 minutes, or until tender. Beats fried chicken. Well, almost.

I have mentioned your Uncle Harry's dog, Sam. He is almost a fully-fledged postal employee. He knows all the routes. Friday Harry carried a west side route. He had Sam with him, but Sam strayed away. Harry went to a mailbox to pick up and he had forgotten his key. He had to walk up to the post office and Melvin, another employee, drove him back. Melvin asked Harry where he left Sam. Harry said he'd left a note on the mailbox for Sam. The note said, "Sam, wait here for me." Melvin was skeptical but when they got back, there sat Sam waiting patiently under the note on the mailbox, so Melvin could only think he had read the note.

There is mixed news on the financial front. The good news is that your Uncle Bill got on a crew at the cemetery digging graves. The problem with that is that he is paid on a piecework basis and Alexandria seems to have been hit with a plague of good health lately, for nobody has died in ages, so we have been pretty poor. Someone did die last week but they sent him over to Summitville for burial. That just makes me so mad I could spit, as they never send us any of theirs. But things are looking up. I was down at the Thriftway this morning and Zelma told me that Fred Thompson's father was ailing and not expected to recover. Also, several of the citizenry looked on their last legs to me, so we will be dining high off the hog 'ere long.

I am about to wind down and think I'll go and get my second cup of coffee. I think of us out there in California, having our coffee and doing our early morning settin' together. On a back cupboard I saw that cup you used to use out there and nearly wept. I am getting to be a silly old woman.

I am sending some Indiana Autumn leaves that I picked up sitting on my back step the other day. I also send my undying devotion, for I love you more than tongue can tell.

Your doting Grandmother

BREAKFASTS & BEVERAGES

NEW-FASHIONED BUCKWHEAT CAKES

August 7, 1964

My Dear One,

I've been trying for days and days to write you. Plenty of time but such dreadful inertia. I've been up since five this morning and have had two buckwheat cakes and two cups of coffee. I'm just about to go get another. Never drink two cups in under 20 minutes. Your taste for the second will be dulled. I read that somewhere. Mama made her buckwheat cakes the old-fashioned way, with cake yeast, which is actually better than the ones I had this morning. But these were quite tasty, nevertheless. Here's how to make them.

2 cups buckwheat flour
1 teaspoon salt
1 teaspoon baking powder
1 teaspoon soda
About 2 ½ cups sour milk or buttermilk

Put flour in bowl and add salt, baking powder and soda. Mix well then stir in the buttermilk slowly until you have a medium thick consistency, but not too thick. Ladle a couple of tablespoons onto a hot, but not smoking skillet or griddle. Watch for little bubbles all over. Then turn down the heat a bit and turn over the cakes. Don't touch the cakes after turning (only the once) as that makes them heavy.

HOOSIER HYSTERIA WAFFLES

March 20, 1960

My Dearie,

I did not intend to let so much time pass before I answered your letter, but pass it has. It is Hoosier Hysteria time (as the papers dub it) once again. Helen said Waller won over $500 betting against Muncie Central. They had not lost a game this year but lost in the final to the Senators of East Chicago. The Senators beat Fort Wayne Central in the afternoon in a heartbreaker game, 62-61.

The night after you called me, I was reading in bed when your grandfather made a dreadful noise and looked just terrible. I immediately called the doctor who said he had had a cerebral reflex, whatever that means. He didn't seem terribly worried and Perry has been fine ever since, eating like a ditcher and humming and singing. This morning I decided to encourage this by making his favorite waffles.

2 cups sifted cake flour
1 tablespoon sugar
2 teaspoons baking powder
½ teaspoon baking soda
½ teaspoon salt
3 eggs, separated
1/3 cup melted butter or oil
1 ½ cup buttermilk

Sift the dry ingredients together. Beat egg whites and yolks separately. Combine oil, beaten egg yolks and buttermilk and add to dry ingredients. Mix well. Fold in stiffly beaten egg whites and pour onto hot waffle iron and cook until golden brown.

Perry downed these like a starving man, so think he must be a great deal better.

DUTCH BABIES

Your Aunt Norma has decided to add the culinary arts to her bag of domestic tricks. She is a whiz-bang housekeeper, a gene that I suspect is missing in our family. Jack likes to tease her by moving something ever so slightly when she leaves a room—say a lamp—by two or three inches. When she walks back in, she all unsuspectingly spies it, and automatically moves it back to its accustomed spot and then carries on to wherever she was headed. That tickles Jack no end. I'm glad he is so easily entertained.

She is no great shakes in the cooking department, however. Doesn't like to dirty the kitchen, I fear. But she has vowed to become a cook and to that end, invited me over for "brunch" (her word) and presented me with Dutch Babies, which she had found in one of her magazines—not Photoplay. She does like to keep up with the doings of the stars. They were actually very nice—the Babies, not the stars—so I asked her for the recipe and include herewith:

1/3 cup butter
4 eggs
1 cup milk
1 cup flour
1 tablespoon sugar
¾ cup powdered sugar

Heat the oven to 450. Melt the butter in a large skillet. Blend the rest of the ingredients in the blender, except the powdered sugar. Pour into the skillet and bake for 20 minutes. Be prepared for a surprise! Sprinkle with sifted powdered sugar. She served them with applesauce and maple syrup.

I've a mind to begin entertaining at brunch, which she held at about 11:00 AM. That seems a nice time to have folks over, though I never have anyone but the family and the Pinochle Club and once in a great while the Democrats or the Rebekahs and none of the above seems to want to eat at any time but afternoon or evening. Well, I actually have the neighbors over, as well, so I guess I do have a lot of people to cook for.

GOOD OLE' PANCAKES

I was making pancakes this morning and felt such a pang in my heart. I remember Keri Jo smacking her lips and saying, "Good ole pancakes. I love pancakes, Ganu. Made me want to make pancakes for her everyday. I do miss you all so and can't wait to see you. Tell Keri Jo that Ganu sends her undying love and will make her good ole pancakes when you get here. I remember her sitting on my lap and listening raptly to "Little Orphant Annie." She's a darling! Give little Craig a hug or two from his lovin' Ganu.

2 cups flour
½ teaspoon salt
1 ½ teaspoon baking soda
1 tablespoon sugar
2 eggs

2 cups sour milk or buttermilk
1 ½ tablespoons melted butter
½ cup chopped pecans

Sift flour, salt, soda and sugar together. Beat eggs until light and add milk then add gradually to the dry ingredients. Beat until smooth and add melted butter. Mix in pecans. Heat and oil your frying pan. If you have a griddle, use that. Pour in batter to make about a 4-or 5-inch pancake. When you see bubbles all around the edges, turn over. Serve with maple syrup or preserves.

LOW BREAD

When Jess and I went out to California that year to visit my brother Will, she would make this for us for breakfast. It's sort of like French toast, but she, for reasons I never knew and forgot to ask her, called it Low Bread. I think it's better than French toast, though very similar.

1 egg
1/8 teaspoon salt
¾ tablespoon sugar
¼ cup milk
½ teaspoon vanilla
4-5 slices of bread

Heat oven to 400. Beat egg and add salt, sugar, milk and vanilla. Pour into shallow dish and dip bread slices into liquid. Try to let bread absorb liquid. Place on greased pan and put in oven until brown. I like to put honey and butter on it but I suppose you could put syrup if you like.

EGG AND CHEESE TOAST

August 29, 1967

My Dear,

I am going to write this with one eye, with the other cocked to the TV, whence Easy Money is playing, as it does not require my full attention. I must watch, however, as it is a local give-away program and at present the total is $930, which I could sorely use.

I do not hold with parents trying to dictate what vocation their children choose, but if Sammy chooses barbering, I would definitely try to discourage him if I were you. He has no real gift, judging from the escaped convict look he achieved with his efforts on his little sister. I am surprised she sat still for it, as I believe she will brook no interference from anyone about her choice of a vocation or anything else. Their foray into barbering reminds me of the time they discovered black paste shoe polish and lovingly painted each other with it. You scrubbed them with cleansing powder, which brought their skin to a pale gray. It makes me laugh to think about it. I wonder why it is that kids can cooperate so well in their naughtiness, but squabble so over tiny things other times.

Four more calls not claimed, which brings Easy Money to $970 and once again they haven't called me. I'm disgusted with it. I'm going to switch it off and have a late breakfast this morning. I will make some egg and cheese toast. Feed this to the children and perhaps they will desist from further mischief. Or not.

3 eggs, beaten lightly
¼ teaspoon salt

Dash pepper
¼ cup milk
1 tablespoon butter
4 slices toast
½ cup grated cheese
Ketchup

Combine eggs, salt pepper and milk. Melt butter in a double boiler, pour in egg mixture and cook. In the bottom pan, keep the water just at the boiling point. Make sure you stir constantly to keep from sticking.

When eggs are cooked through, spread toast with ketchup, pile on scrambled eggs and cover with the cheese. (I like American cheese but I also like to use a sharp cheddar for your Uncle Jack). Place in broiler and let the cheese melt and brown. Serve this while it's hot!

DRIED BEEF GRAVY—NAVY STYLE

Nar-de-gar magazines—that's those with lofty aspirations—call this Creamed Chipped Beef. When your Uncle Harry came back from the Navy, he called it something else—to do with a shingle, but I wouldn't put that in a recipe for my granddaughter.

Package of dried beef
Hunk of butter, maybe 1 tablespoon or more
2 tablespoons flour, more or less
2 cups milk.
Salt and pepper to taste

Take the dried beef—it used to come in little glasses, which we then used for jelly—shred and frizzle it in a skillet with the hunk of butter.

Don't cook it too long; it's already dry. Then add flour to equal the amount of butter, stir it for a minute or so till it's incorporated, then slowly add a couple of cups of milk, more or less, stirring the while till thickened. This won't need much salt as the beef's already salty, but pepper nicely. Serve over biscuits or toast.

You used to love this for Sunday breakfast when you would stay with me. I wish I could make it for you now.

RINKTUM DITTY

Been having some trouble with my new teeth and. I'm hoping not to lose any weight while I wait to have them settled in. I can still reach around the big part of my right arm with my thumb and middle finger of the left touching, so I know I'm not very fat yet. I want to maintain what I have of this portliness, so I've been making things that go down without excess chewing. This sounds like it might be an Irish dish, but believe it is actually English. I like the name.

1 tablespoon butter
1 small finely chopped onion
2 cups diced or crushed tomatoes
1 teaspoon salt
¼ teaspoon pepper
2 teaspoons sugar
½ lb grated American cheese
1 egg, beaten
Several slices buttered toast

In a medium frying pan, melt the butter and cook the onion until soft, but not browned. Add the tomatoes, salt, pepper and sugar and heat completely. Add cheese and cook until melted stirring constantly. Add egg slowly, stirring constantly and cook for 1 minute more. Serve on buttered toast.

SORE LOSER COFFEE CAKE

November 18, 1962

My Dear,

Did you hear that our own Birch Bayh beat Homer Capeheart? I was quite elated. Glad too that Richard (Nixon) did not make it. He was not a very good loser. Capeheart wasn't either. I was to bring something to the Democrat Club the other day and brought my old standby Bisquick coffee cake, for it is easy to make and tasty into the bargain. No one objected. Still too pumped up over the election results, I imagine.

Cake:
1 egg
½ cup sugar
¼ cup vegetable oil
1 ½ cup Bisquick
¾ cup milk

Set oven at 375. Mix above ingredients until well moistened. Pour into a well-greased 8 x 8 pan.

Topping:
1 ½ teaspoon cinnamon
1 teaspoon vegetable oil or butter
¼ cup tightly packed brown sugar
½ cup chopped nuts.

Stir together, sprinkle crumbly mixture over cake and bake for 30 minutes. Goes well with a good cup of coffee.

CINNAMON TOAST

When I was sick last week, Perry took care of me. He was sweet and solicitous of my comfort. Unfortunately, he was also the cook and his repertoire consists mainly of toast. We had toast with butter and then butter with toast. We had it with and without jelly. Once we had it under pork and beans. And then for dessert we had cinnamon toast. I am glad I am better and am temporarily swearing off toast. But if you're not, the children might like our dessert.

Put equal parts sugar and cinnamon in a shaker. Make toast and butter it. Shake cinnamon/sugar mixture over it. Slide under the broiler for a few minutes, watching carefully lest it burn. Take out, slice into toast "soldiers," and serve with hot cocoa.

REAL COCOA

My Dearie,

Today it's snowing. That's one of those things that I have mixed feelings about. It's a delight to the eye as long as I'm looking at it from the front window. But it's treacherous underfoot and, as I'm none too steady in that department, think I'll spend the day inside. It's also cold. The other day your granddad asked me, "Would you rather be cold or hungry?" Glad I didn't have to choose, but both of us knew we'd choose hungry any day over cold.

On cold days when I was little, and for many years after I wasn't so little, Mama used to give me cocoa and buttered toast. I know they have those mixes for making cocoa, but here's how she made it and how I still do:

2 tablespoons cocoa
2 tablespoons sugar
Dash of salt
1 cup water
3 cups milk
1 teaspoon vanilla
4 marshmallows

Mix cocoa, sugar, salt and water in a small saucepan and bring to a boil over low heat. Boil for a couple of minutes, stirring the while. Then add the milk and heat. Don't let it boil. Take it off the stove and stir in the vanilla. Then carefully pour into cups and add a marshmallow to each cup.

This makes enough for four cups and is it ever so warming on a wintry day with buttered toast accompanying. Or your granddad likes graham crackers with his.

BERTHA'S HOT CHOCOLATE

Annie's sister Bertha, who married her husband Arthur when she was well into her sixties, makes it like this:

1 ½ squares (1 ½ ounces) unsweetened chocolate
¾ cup water
2 ½ tablespoons sugar
Dash salt
2 ¼ cups milk
1 teaspoon vanilla

Cook the chocolate and water together in a bowl over a saucepan with simmering water, (it's how she makes a double boiler) stirring constantly until melted. Add sugar and salt and bring to boil for 4 or 5 minutes, still stirring. Gradually add milk continuing to stir. Then add vanilla and beat with an eggbeater till frothy. Pour over a marshmallow into each of four cups. Or have two for yourself.

I think her version's a lot more trouble than mine, but is admittedly tasty, as your Aunt Norma would say.

EASIEST HOT CHOCOLATE

Here's the easiest one of all, barring that instant stuff that is available, but is an abomination of nature. I say this despite my love of mixes and anything that makes livin' easy.

4 cups hot milk
1 cup finely chopped semi-sweet chocolate

Pour milk over chocolate; stir well and drink. You can beat it with an eggbeater if you want, but I think that's too much trouble. Don't forget the ubiquitous marshmallow, without which it just ain't hot chocolate.

CHOCOLATE COFFEE

It's snowing outside, glad I'm not. I think I'll just watch the flakes come down and smile smugly knowing that it can't get me. While I'm doing that, I'll probably have some chocolate coffee. Something that your Aunt Jenny used to make me. I fell in love with it. Makes me feel all warm and toasty inside. I made extra so that your Granddaddy can have some when he gets up.

¼ cup chocolate sauce
4 cups hot coffee
½ cup heavy cream

Mix sauce with the hot coffee. Whip the cream and beat into the coffee mixture. Serve hot.

BREADS & BISCUITS

ALEXANDRIA BANANA DATE NUT BREAD

October 5, 1967

My dear,

I think we must be telepathic for your letter was dated 9/27 and that's the day I wrote my little ode to Alison. Was it satisfactory? Tell me what she said about her "pome." Think some of it was a little over her head but you, in your best schoolmarm fashion, could elucidate. She is so darned cute. Smart, too.

I watched the ball game. I am for the Red Sox and if you would ask me why I could not tell you. St. Louis has such a crummy bus station. Never been to Boston. I believe they bake Boston Brown Bread in Boston but have never had it. I do, however have some over-ripe bananas and will put them to use in some banana bread, which is what we bake in Alexandria.

3 very ripe bananas
juice of 1 lemon
1/3 cup cooking oil or butter
½ cup brown sugar
1 ½ cup whole wheat flour
½ teaspoon salt
½ teaspoon baking powder
½ teaspoon baking soda
½ cup wheat germ
1 cup chopped dates
1 cup toasted, chopped nuts

Heat oven to 375. Mash bananas and mix with lemon juice till smooth. Cream butter or oil and sugar together and add banana mix, stirring very well. Sift together flour, salt, baking powder, and baking soda and mix in wheat germ. Add to the banana mix and stir in dates and nuts. (The latter will not sink to the bottom if you dredge them in flour first). The dough will be rather stiff. Turn it out into a greased 4 x 8 loaf pan and bake for about 45 minutes or until a strand of spaghetti, (uncooked, of course) stuck in the middle comes out clean.

MAPLE GINGERBREAD

I resigned from my Pinochle Club last summer when my health was bad but I'm better now. One of the regulars has been sick and I've been playing in her place. I wish she would resign, for I am able to go now, but do not think she will. Unless she dies. But I mayn't get that lucky. In hopes that I would tip the scales toward their preferring me to her, I brought this the last time I played.

1 cup maple syrup
1 beaten egg
1 cup sour cream
2 1/3 cups flour sifted
1 teaspoon baking soda
1 ½ teaspoon powdered ginger
½ teaspoon salt
4 tablespoons melted butter

In a bowl, add syrup, egg and sour cream. Blend together. Sift flour, soda, ginger and salt and stir into mixture. Mix well. Add butter and beat. Pour into a baking pan, lined with waxed paper. Bake in a hot oven (350 degrees) for 30 minutes.

They said nothing but the looks on their faces as they ingested this tells me my chances are good.

BISHOP'S BREAD

April 11, 1967

My Dear,

Been quite some time since I got your letter and I was no end glad, but you know how it is. I just have so much to do that I neglect my correspondence horribly. I hardly ever get my beds made before 7:30 AM and sometimes I have dishes to wash in the morning, so what with my TV programs I just do not have the time—or I'm afraid—the inclination. I used to be a darned good letter writer, too.

I was thinking I might come out again to visit. Don't worry about not having a spare room for me. I won't be bringing much in the way of wardrobe, so will only need a doorknob on which to hang the clothes I'm not wearing and a davenport to sleep on. I could do some baking while there. I think the progeny would enjoy this.

4 eggs, separated
1 cup sugar
1 teaspoon vanilla
1 cup sifted flour
2 teaspoons baking powder
1/8 teaspoon salt
1 cup blanched almonds chopped
1 cup raisins
Powdered Sugar

Beat yolks of eggs until they're lemony colored. Add sugar and beat well. Add vanilla, sift dry flour, baking powder and salt together and stir into the egg mixture. Add the nuts and raisins. Beat egg whites until stiff and fold into the mixture. Pour into a greased oblong pan and bake in a 350-degree oven for about 20 minutes. While still hot sprinkle powdered sugar on top and then cut into squares.

CHEATIN' BISCUITS

I'm not ashamed to say I make Bisquick biscuits, which I know is cheating. When I was learning to cook, we did not have 'mod cons' as the British call them (modern conveniences), and we were only too glad when things like baking mixes became available. Here's the recipe for 'real' biscuits—the kind we made before Bisquick, if you're so inclined.

2 cups flour
3 tablespoons baking powder
Dash salt
4 tbs butter
1 cup milk
flour for surface

Pre-heat the oven to 450 degrees. Blend flour, baking powder and salt in a bowl. Cut in the butter till it looks like cornmeal, then add the milk. When blended, turn out onto a surface that you've sprinkled with more flour and knead for a couple of minutes. Roll ½ inch thick and cut with a cutter—an upturned glass will do. Put on an ungreased cookie sheet and bake for 8 to 10 minutes.

Give the children the extra dough to make treasures and bake them along with your biscuits. They'll be a little gray from over-handling and under-washing, and possibly being dropped on the floor, but tasty, nonetheless. If you lose the recipe, use the one on the Bisquick box. Maybe gourmets can tell the difference, but I can't.

HOOSIER SKILLET CORNBREAD

Nov 24, 1961

My Dear,

In my new apartment I have a lovely big east window in my bedroom and can watch the sun come up if it does. It has been shining brightly during this cold spell but was six below last night. The house is nice and warm though, so you can just write down in your little red book that I am completely contented.

Yesterday I cooked up a mess of beans with ham and made the cornbread your granddad always liked. It is now nearly a year that he's been gone, and I miss him something dreadful, but try to concentrate on remembering the many years I spent with that quiet, kind man. As often as not, I succeed, though this wasn't the case a few months ago.

I don't usually measure when I cook, but with baked goods it can be a little tricky not to, so I'm giving more exact measures than is my habit.

2 eggs
1 cup milk
¼ cup melted butter or oil
1 cup flour
1 cup corn meal

1 tsp salt
3 tsp baking powder
2 tbs sugar

Preheat oven to 400 degrees. Beat the eggs and milk together in a bowl. Add butter or oil. In another bowl, mix all the dry ingredients. Pour the wet ingredients into the dry and mix until moist. You could pour this into a greased square pan, but I've never used anything but a black, cast-iron skillet. I personally think that's the secret of success for cornbread. Bake for about 25 minutes or until golden brown.

Papa always used to crumble up leftover cornbread in a glass, add cold buttermilk and eat with a spoon, sometimes with a little sugar. He said it was heavenly stuff.

JOHNNYCAKES

Mama used to make Johnnycakes. I loved them. A Johnnycake is so simple to make. It was originally called a "journeycake" because it was frequently made by travelers because it was so quickly and easily made. Mama told me that corn meal was mixed with water or even snow and baked over the fire.

2 cups corn meal
4 cups boiling water
2 teaspoon salt
1 tablespoon Crisco

Mix corn meal and salt, add boiling water and shortening and beat well. Spread to about ½ in thick on a greased baking pan. Bake in oven at 350 degrees until crisp, about 35 to 45 minutes. Makes 2 cakes about 8 inches in diameter. This can be baked on a greased griddle rather than in the oven.

SPOON BREAD

I used to love to watch Mama cook. Sometimes when Papa was at work and it was just Mama and me, I'd sit and watch and marvel at how she could take apparently nothing and make it into something wonderful. If I played my cards right, and I usually did, I'd get to lick the bowl if it was something sweet. I loved to watch her make spoon bread too. I didn't lick the spoon, but it was still a marvel to watch.

2 cups white corn meal
2 cups boiling water
1 teaspoon salt
3 tablespoons melted butter
1 ½ cup milk
3 eggs

Set oven to 350 degrees. Sift corn meal about 3 times. Mix with boiling water. Make sure there are no lumps. Add salt, butter and milk. Separate eggs. Beat yolks until light and separately beat whites until they form peaks but are not dry. Add yolks and whites to corn meal mixture, slowly while mixing. Pour into a buttered baking dish and bake for 45 minutes.

PARKER HOUSE ROLLS

The ladies at Pinochle Club absolutely love it when I make rolls. I always bring some in. I love it too! And as a bonus for me, my house smells heavenly when I make them. I remember the times you would all come in and comment on the wonderful aroma if I had just made them.

2 tablespoon butter or Crisco
1 teaspoon salt
¼ cup sugar
1 cake yeast
1 ½ cup lukewarm water
3 ½ cups flour, sifted
1 egg, beaten

Add shortening, salt, sugar and crumbled yeast cake to water. Stir until butter is melted. Stir in sifted flour, cover and set in a warm place to rise. (Sometimes I put the dough into an oven with a pan of hot water on a lower shelf). When the dough has doubled in size, add egg. Knead and let rise again to double again. Roll out about ½ inches thick on board with lots of flour on it. Cut with a biscuit cutter (about 2 inches in diameter). Crease in the center with a dull knife. Brush with melted butter and fold over, pinching the dough at the sides to make a pocketbook. Brush tops of rolls with more melted butter. Let rise and bake on a cookie sheet in a hot oven at 400 degrees for about 20 minutes. Should make about 2 dozen rolls.

MURDER WEAPON BREAD
Salt Rising Bread

Perry was so extremely fond of salt rising bread that, early when we were married, I decided to bake some. The results were less than stellar. I still don't know what I did wrong, but that bread was so heavy and hard when it came out of the oven, that it would have caused dire harm should someone be hit with it.

When Perry saw it, he slumped down at the table and bowed his head. I wasn't sure what was happening—maybe he was praying? Then I saw his shoulders begin to shake and he looked up at me with tears streaming, he was laughing so hard and trying not to show it lest he hurt my feelings, which of course he did. I got mad, which tickled him even more but finally that tickled me. I told him I could kill him with it, and it would be the perfect crime, as I could grate it into breadcrumbs and they'd never find the murder weapon.

I never really did learn to make salt rising bread, as it is pretty tricky, but here is the recipe that Jenny always used. Maybe you'll have better luck than I did.

Sponge:
1 cup milk
1 tablespoon sugar
½ cup cornmeal
1 teaspoon salt
2 cups lukewarm water

Dough
½ teaspoon baking soda
1 tablespoon lukewarm water
2 cups flour

3 tablespoons shortening
2 tablespoons sugar
6 cups flour

Heat the milk. Stir in sugar, cornmeal and 1 teaspoon of salt. Put in a jar and put in your electric skillet that has a bit of water in it and is set to about 105 to 115 degrees. Leave it to ferment overnight or till it is bubbly and has that "salt-rising" aroma.

Dissolve the baking soda in 1 tablespoon of lukewarm water and add to the sponge you've created with the fermenting. Stir in 5 ¼ cups of flour. Knead in more flour as necessary to keep it from sticking. Knead for about 10 minutes until it is smooth and elastic. Cut the dough into 3 parts. Shape into loaves and place in 3 greased bread pans. Place in a warm oven at about 85 degrees. In about 5 hours or so the bread will rise 2 ½ time original size and will round up out of the top of the pans.

Heat the oven to 375 and bake for 10 minutes. Then reduce the temperature of the oven to 350 degrees and bake for another 20 minutes till golden brown.

If you're as lucky as I was you won't need a rolling pin to bash your husband when he sneaks in late, like they do in the funny papers.

WASHDAY BREAD

When I was about 12, I went out to West Virginia to spend the summer with my brother Sam and his wife Katherine, whom I found to be rather stern, but Sam could always make her smile. One evening he told this story about Papa and his bad eyes. Like all us Montgomery's, Papa was severely nearsighted. So, one day when Sam knew Papa'd be coming home, he cut through the cornfields and was sitting on a fence when Papa drove his horse and buggy by. Sam waved and called out, "How'do, Mr. Montgomery," to which Papa responded, "How'do, young man." Whereupon Sam ran lickety-split through the fields twice more and repeated this entire transaction. He said when Papa got home, he told Mama that three of the nicest boys had spoken politely to him on his way home. This tickled Sam no end, and Katherine's mouth quirked up at the corner when he told the story. Even at age 12 I knew that, while Papa hadn't been able to see who Sam was, he knew him by his voice. But I didn't want to spoil Sam's story.

Katherine was rather a fine cook, though and made wonderful bread. She called this her washday bread because it takes so little watching and can be made up and be rising while you do your wash.

3 ¾ cups flour
1 heaping teaspoon salt
½ cake yeast (or ½ teaspoon granular yeast)
1 ½ cup lukewarm milk

Fill the washtub with water and put it on to boil. This is for the clothes, of course.

Then put the flour and salt into a large bowl. Dissolve the yeast in the milk and add to the dry ingredients. Stir with a wooden spoon till all comes together. Turn it out onto a floured board and knead, folding the dough over, pushing it away from you and turn it a quarter turn and repeat till it feels springy. Roll it in flour and put it in a warm bowl, covering with a clean tea towel out of drafts. Forget about it while you do the wash.

When everything's ready to hang on the line, come in and punch the dough down, knead well again, roll in flour and forget about it while you hang out the clothes, which won't take as long as washing them, thus giving you a longer first rising, shorter second. When you're done, come in and punch the dough down again, give it a final kneading and shape it into a loaf. Slash four cuts with a sharp (clean) razor and brush with water. Turn the oven on to 450 and brew yourself a cup of tea while you wait for the loaf to proof. After you've had a cup of tea, put the loaf into the oven for half hour. Turn oven down to 425 and bake another twenty minutes.

If you're using a modern washer and dryer instead of a scrub board, you might want to go shopping while the wash is tumbling to give the bread time to rise.

COURTIN' POTATO BREAD

March 9, 1968

My Dearest,

I had my first date with your Granddaddy 56 years ago tonight, which is apropos of nothing, but writing the date reminded me. He was the kindest person I ever knew, despite his propensity for tidiness. I really thought I might leave him the time I came home with a birthday card I'd just purchased and left it in its sack on the table while I went to hang up my coat. When I returned, the card had disappeared and after a lengthy search I discovered it torn neatly in half in the wastebasket. He'd seen the "trash" lying on the table and neatened up. I could've killed him, but thankfully didn't.

As a spinster of nigh onto 29 years, I was still living at home with Mama and Papa and this bread was in the oven when Perry came to walk out with me. It smelled so heavenly I think it made me more alluring than I might otherwise have appeared to him. You've already snared a man, so you won't need this kind of help, but it's good to eat even if you don't.

2 cups potato water
1 cake yeast
2 tablespoons Crisco
2 tablespoons sugar
1 tablespoon salt
6 cups sifted flour

Cook 3 potatoes in boiling water until tender and mash into water. Heat 2 cups of potato water until lukewarm. Break up cake of yeast into ¼ cup of the water. To the rest of the water, add Crisco, sugar and salt. Add to mixture, softened yeast and ½ the flour. Beat, gradually adding the remaining flour. Place on floured board and knead until elastic. Place in a bowl and let rise in warm place. When it's double in size, divide in two parts. Shape into loaf shapes and place into greased loaf pans. Let rise again until double in size. Bake in pre-heated oven at 375 degrees for 45 minutes or until bread pulls from side of pan.

SALADS, SOUPS & VEGETABLES

KATIE'S PINEAPPLE BOAT

My Dear One:

The sun is shining, and it has the promise of a bright sunny day, albeit a bit nippy. All in all, very pretty to look at. I shan't be out in it so won't mind the nip in the air. Slept in this morning as I had a rather late night. Gallivanting about. I went to Pinochle Club last night. It was a carry-in. I carried mine in, as did all the others. Some people are so artistic with their food. Mine, while tasty, lacks a little in presentation. Katie May brought a fruit salad that was very pretty. She had carved out a pineapple and filled it with fruit. Quite impressive! Also, quite good. Some had brought canapés that looked as though they had been from a magazine. A great time was had by all.

I went to the store yesterday to purchase the ingredients for my carry-in. The girl behind the cash register asked if I had bought everything I came for. I told her that I had considered a bit of snuff, as I had never tried it. I do believe in trying new things. She thought that quite comical. I almost meant it.

My little dog Jeco is lying asleep beside me in the warmth of the sun. He is such good company for me. Hope this finds you and your loved ones well. I do miss you all so.

1 large, well-shaped pineapple
1 cup blueberries
1 cup strawberries
½ cup raspberries
2 ripe bananas, sliced
Whipped cream

Scoop out the pineapple in pieces to be used in the salad. Fill with all the fruit. Pile high, using any fruit desired. Top with whipped cream just before serving.

NO COMPLAINING SPLIT PEA SOUP

Not everybody is crazy about split pea soup, but they mustn't say so in my presence when I cook it. I heard a story about a group of men who would go hunting each fall and stay in a cabin in the woods for a few days, each taking a turn at the cooking. They established a rule that if someone complained about the cooking, that person then assumed the cooking duties out of turn. One morning one of them began to drink his coffee, sputtered a bit and cried, "Damnation, that coffee's strong!" Then remembering himself, added, "But by Gawd I like it that way!"

3 cups dried split peas
1 cup diced ham
1 medium onion, diced
2 carrots, sliced
1 tablespoon Worcestershire sauce
½ teaspoon garlic powder
2 quarts water or broth
        (this is where you can use that potato water)
Salt & pepper to taste

Steal a large pot away from catching leaky roof drippings and wash it thoroughly. Combine all ingredients in said pot and simmer for 2 to 3 hours, stirring once in a while. Cook till peas disintegrate. Wonderful stuff. Warms your innards.

HYGENIC CORN CHOWDER

Years ago—1912 to be exact—my dear friend Jess and I traveled out to California to visit my brother Will. They later married, though she was many years his junior. She says they had a lovely 28-year love affair until he died, so the age difference didn't seem to interfere. We took our time traveling and stayed in various hotels and rooming houses along the way. In one of the latter we knew they had high standards for hygiene, as there was a comb securely chained to one side of the bathroom sink and a toothbrush to the other side. Apparently, they'd had problems with folks purloining these toilet articles for their continued personal use—thus the chains. We availed ourselves of neither.

However, they did offer a nice bill of fare, including a delicious corn chowder. When Jess and I arrived at Will's, we experiment-ed to duplicate the recipe and came up with this one, which, if memory serves, is very close to what we ate there.

8 or 10 slices bacon
1 chopped onion
4 large potatoes, peeled and cubed
2 cups water
2 cups heavy cream
1 teaspoon sugar
1 tablespoon butter
8 cups corn, off the cob or frozen
3 teaspoons salt
½ teaspoon pepper
4 cups milk

Slice bacon into small bits and fry in a large soup pot until crisp. Remove bacon and drain, pouring off the fat but leave a film on the bottom of the pot for flavor. Put onion, potatoes and water into the pot and bring to a boil, then simmer about 15 minutes till potatoes are firm but tender.

In another smaller pan combine cream, sugar, butter and corn. Simmer over low heat while the potatoes cook. Then add to the potato mixture along with salt pepper and milk. Heat all but don't boil. *Lip smackin' good.*

JENNY'S GREEN SOUP

October 17, 1964

My Dearie,

Today would be my sister Jenny's 90ᵗʰ birthday. She was 10 years older than I. She was always a very responsible person and I don't think she had much fun in life. I was the youngest, so she and my other brothers and sisters spoiled me, I fear. She always let me know she thought I was pretty special. I miss her.

She and Frank had that great passel of children and were always poor as Job's Turkey, so she grew a large vegetable garden to help feed the family. Here is a soup she used to cook to use up the greens she grew in gay profusion in that plot. I'm not ordinarily fond of cooked greens but fixed this way they're quite tasty. I think she made it in greater amounts, but I've scaled it down for a smaller family.

1 onion or bunch of scallions
1 tablespoon oil or butter

2 to 4 potatoes, peeled and chopped
Broth to cover potatoes
6-8 cups of any greens: chard, kale, collards, spinach or even lettuce
Milk
Salt and pepper to taste

Saute the onion in oil or butter until soft. Add potatoes and cover with broth. Cook until tender and then add greens, simmering until they wilt. Jenny put all this through a food mill, but you could blend it and then put it back in the pot. Add more broth if too thick. Add a small amount of milk to make it creamy. Salt and pepper.

GERITOL TOMATO AND BAKED BEAN SOUP

I've been so peppy lately. I walked down to Harry's and they were not home, so I went on down to Annie's and then walked to Kane's and she fetched me back home. I scared myself this week with all I have done. I cleaned the closet, this room, the back porch and the icebox. I got me 100 Geritols and have taken about half of them, thus the extraordinary energy, maybe. However, it is now time to fix some dinner and am feeling lazy so will make this soup, which is so easy.

1 ½ cup cold baked beans
1 stalk celery diced
1 tablespoon diced onion
3 cups water
2 cups cooked tomatoes
1 tablespoon melted butter
1 tablespoon flour
Salt and pepper to taste

Combine beans, celery, onion and water and simmer for about 30 minutes, until the vegetables are soft. Add the tomatoes and push through a strainer. Melt the butter add flour and mix well. Add to the strained vegetables. Add salt and pepper. Heat to boiling point, remove from heat and serve.

SOAP OPERA BARLEY SOUP

My sister Jenny is such a sad individual. I'm not sure why. All of her children are out of the house and heaven knows that should be a relief. Or maybe that's the problem. At any rate, I used to go over about the time that the soap operas came on the radio and make her listen to them with me to see that some folks have it far worse than she. No one was more miserable than Stella Dallas. She did love for me to come even though I made her listen. She would often make this soup, which we'd have while we listened to it and commiserated with Stella. Sometimes that would even make her sort of giggle.

½ cup Barley
1 qt boiling water
1 teaspoon salt
2 cups vegetable stock or beef stock.
½ cup Diced Celery
½ cup Diced Onions
½ cup Diced Carrots
1 mango (ed. bell pepper)
Salt and Pepper to taste

Rinse Barley in cold water and cook in salted boiling water until tender (about 2 hours). When water has evaporated, add stock. Celery, onions, diced carrots and diced bell pepper boiled with the soup makes for a wonderful flavor. I'd cook them at a simmer for about an hour.

RUMBLED POTATO SOUP

I was about to peel some potatoes to make this soup, which is my favorite, when I thought of a funny story Harry told me some time back while he still had the H & H. Lee, who was about 12 or 13 at the time, had come to work there and was put in charge of the "rumbler," which is an old-fashioned machine Harry had that peeled potatoes for the French fries. The way it worked was that it had a large revolving bowl with rough, grater-like sides. The potatoes were put inside it and when it was switched on, the potatoes rumbled around until the peels were eventually scraped off. Most of them, that is. When you took the potatoes out, they still had bits of peel and eyes to cut out by hand with a knife.

Well, Lee went through that process once, and while digging out the eyes with a paring knife, a light went on for him. Time-and-motion-study expert that he fancied himself, he decided he'd eliminate the onerous last step by the simple expedient of leaving the rumbler on longer than the suggested time. Which he did. Well, you can imagine the result—strangely shaped, marble-sized potatoes emerged. Lee was somewhat abashed and Harry, who was appalled at the waste of potatoes, was nevertheless sufficiently tickled that he didn't bother to go through the motions of a rant about waste. We both thought it was pretty funny when he told me about it.

4 tablespoons butter
2 leeks, chopped
1 small onion, finely chopped
3 or 4 good-sized russet potatoes
3 ¼ cups broth (chicken or vegetable)
Salt and pepper to taste

Peel and chop the potatoes into small pieces. Heat half the butter in a large heavy pan and sauté the onions and leeks over medium-low heat for about 7 minutes, stirring occasionally. You want them softened, not browned. Add the potatoes to the pan and cook for 2 or 3 minutes, still stirring occasionally. Add the broth and bring all to a boil, then reduce the heat and simmer gently for a half hour or so till the vegetables are very tender. Add salt and pepper, or you can leave it out and let people salt their own at the table.

You could serve it like this or blend it or just mash a few of the potatoes into the soup, which is the way I do it. This will make you well if you're sick and keep you well if you're not.

FROZEN PEACH AND PECAN SALAD

My Dear

I found this recipe in a magazine and I tried it. It made me think of you. I don't know which you always loved the most, my apple dumplings or my peach pie. I wish you could have been here to share it with me. Your Grandfather didn't care for it. He said it was too cold, but I knew that you would care greatly for it. Carl had brought me some fresh peaches from his back yard and I put them to good use.

37

4 peaches, peeled and halved
1 cup Miracle Whip
1 cup cream cheese
1 cup chopped pecans
1 cup whipping cream, whipped

Arrange peach halves, hollow side up in tray. Mix cream cheese, Miracle Whip, pecans and whipped cream together and pour over peaches. Freeze for about 3 or 4 hours. I served it over lettuce. Very pretty and very good.

TOOTHSOME CUCUMBER JELLO SALAD

Your grandfather was uncommonly fond of this salad, so I made it pretty often. I recollect the Christmas when we started to sit down to dinner and Perry remembered he hadn't his teeth in. It was his habit to take them out from time to time and deposit them in the breast pocket of his shirt. When asked why, he'd pat the pocket and say, "Restin' my mouth." But he had not done that this time and they were nowhere to be found. At last we discovered them smiling down at us from the top of the piano. He was delighted, for cucumbers are difficult to eat with just the gums. Oh, don't we all miss him so?

1 small package lime Jello
¾ cup hot water
¼ cup lemon juice
8 or 10 scallions, chopped fine
1 cup sour cream
2 unpeeled cucumbers, chopped

Mix Jello with water and lemon juice and put in ice box for ½ hour or till it starts to thicken. Add scallions, sour cream and cucumber and put back in to chill until set.

TOOTHLESS ORANGE PINEAPPLE SALAD

This was another salad Granddaddy liked. It is far easier to eat than the other one if you've misplaced your teeth.

2 packages orange Jello
1 ½ cups boiling water
1 8 ounce can Mandarin oranges with juice
1 small can frozen orange juice
1 tall can chunk pineapple with juice
1 cup cold water

Pour the boiling water over Jello in a bowl to dissolve. Add frozen orange juice, cold water, and the juices and put in ice box to thicken for about a half hour or so. Add pineapple chunks and oranges and put back in to chill until set. *Then serve and gum away!*

MR MICAWBER'S PEA SALAD

I have gone out and bought my provender for the week and when I count what is left of my munificent monthly funds, I find myself rather short. I was trying to take Mr. Micawber's attitude about it and force myself to believe, "Something will turn up." But in case it doesn't, have been contemplating getting a slouch hat and a mask, wearing Bill's trousers and sticking up a tavern. I don't think they'd know me in Bill's size 47" pants, but fear they'd recognize me by my stagger. A risky undertaking in a small town. I was, however, able to afford a can of peas so think I'll make pea salad.

2 strips bacon
1 (14 ounce) can peas
couple of celery stalks, chopped
couple of scallions, chopped
¼ cup sour cream
¼ cup Miracle Whip
½ cup nuts (cashews, pecans, etc)
if you've got them.

Fry the bacon crisp, blot on paper towels and crumble. Drain peas (I'm not going to get into a debate over canned or frozen. You can use frozen if you like—just run boiling water over a package of them). Combine peas, celery, scallions, sour cream and Miracle Whip and chill. Just before serving, stir in the bacon bits and nuts. I like cashews. Salt and pepper to taste. Your mother puts little cubes of Velveeta in hers. You could do that, I guess, but I never do.

Maybe I could go into the catering business and wouldn't have to rob a tavern. I never looked so good in a slouch hat, anyway.

Ed. Note: Dickens was high on Grandmother's reading list. Mr. Micawber was a character she was fond of in "David Copperfield." He had a large family but no means to support them. Nevertheless, he was always optimistic that something would "turn up." You'll have to read the book to find out if it ever did. You'll be glad you did. At the very least watch the movie that features W.C. Fields as the best Mr. Micawber ever on film. What a treat!

NEW YEAR'S LUCKY PEAS

My brother Will always told me to "Eat peas on New Year's Day and you'll have plenty of everything for the whole year." I don't know if that's true because I don't always eat them on New Year's Day. However, I seem to have the same amount of everything on the years I do and the years I don't. Still, I do like black-eyed peas and have them on occasion even on off days. In the south they call this Hoppin' John. Good whatever you call it.

2 cups black-eyed peas
¼ pound salt pork or ham
2 cups cooked rice
2 tablespoons butter
Salt and pepper to taste

Soak peas overnight in water to cover plus a bit more. Pour off soaking water, add fresh water to cover and cook with salt pork or ham until peas are tender. There should be only a small bit of liquid left on them. Add cooked rice and season with salt pepper and butter. Simmer for about 15 minutes. I like to serve mine with corn bread or just bread and butter.

COUSIN HAZEL'S BEAN SALAD

My cousin Hazel, well actually she's my niece—she's my sister Jenny's oldest girl, but pretty close to my age so I've always called her cousin—always brings this to potlucks

1 (14 ounce) can kidney beans, rinsed
4 or 5 scallions

½ cup chopped cucumber pickles
1 carrot (optional)
½ red bell pepper, chopped (optional)
½ cup Miracle Whip
2 tablespoons pickle juice

Chop the scallions and throw into a casserole dish with the beans. Chop up the pickles. Some people use gherkins, but Hazel swears by good ol' bread and butter cucumber pickles. Grate the carrot if you're using it and about half a pepper chopped. We've always called them mangoes, but I guess you call them peppers out there. You said in Australia they called them capsicums. You get the drift. Anyway, mix this up with the Miracle Whip thinned with pickle juice. Hazel's salad always varies depending on whether she's been to the store or just used what she had on hand. Very tasty.

RED MACARONI AND MINNAISE SALAD

I seldom use Miracle Whip that I don't think of you and your "minnaise sandwiches." You used to head for the kitchen about as soon as you got to my house, make a Miracle Whip sandwich—just Miracle Whip and bread—and then head to the desk to hunt for treasures.

1 8-ounce box elbow macaroni
½ cup French dressing
2 medium apples
2 tablespoons lemon juice
1 small minced onion
1 cup Miracle Whip
Paprika

Boil macaroni until it's tender. Drain and rinse in cold water. When chilled, add French Dressing and refrigerate for about 2 hours. Peel and dice apples. Add apples, lemon juice, onion and Miracle Whip and add to the macaroni. Before you serve it, sprinkle the top with paprika.

M-M-MASHED POTATOES

Mashed potatoes must surely be manna from the gods. And they are so simple to make. Just peel 2 or 3—or more, depending on how many you are feeding—russet potatoes. Don't use red ones, they're too waxy. Cut them into fourths and plop in boiling water that you turn down to a simmer for 20 minutes or so—till a fork poked in shows them to be sufficiently cooked. Hold the potatoes back with the lid while you pour the cooking water into a jar, which you'll put in the ice box to use to make soup later.

Drop in a healthy (don't believe what they say) knob of butter and start to mash with a non-mechanical masher. Pour in a little heated milk and continue to whip with your electric mixer. Salt and pepper, add another pat of butter and, as the Brits would say, "Bob's your uncle." Or in your case, Bill, Jack or Harry.

ANNIE'S FAVORITE SOUR CREAM POTATO SALAD

Went to visit Annie. She has a bad case of the epizootic. Made her a poultice of dishwater grass and flour and mustard. Placed on the chest, it draws out the bad stuff. Smells to Billy-be-durned but does the job. To find dishwater grass, you must look to where you throw the dishwater out the back door and use some of the grass that grows there.

I also took her some of her favorite potato salad. She may not feel like eating it until the poultice takes effect, but she'll love it when it does.

About 4 good-sized potatoes, peeled, cooked and diced
½ cup chopped celery
¼ cup chopped sweet pickles
1 tablespoon chopped onion
3 hard-boiled eggs, chopped
Dash of salt and pepper
½ cup Miracle Whip
1 ½ cup sour cream
3 tablespoons vinegar
1 teaspoon yellow mustard

Combine potatoes, celery, pickles, onion, eggs, salt and pepper, tossing lightly. Combine the sour cream, Miracle Whip, vinegar and mustard. Mix and refrigerate for about 1 hour for the ingredients to blend. It is so good it may, in fact, ward off the epizootic.

HOT POTATO SALAD

When your dad had that garden in that plot he rented there in Gas City, he used to bring me produce on Sundays when you'd all come down in that old Chevy you had, with you girls and Peppy in the back seat. His potatoes one year were rather a disappointment. He said he had some as big as golf balls and some as big as marbles... and then there were some small ones. That would have been okay for this recipe, as it calls for small ones.

10-12 small potatoes (I like red ones for this)
4 slices bacon
½ lb. pkg. Velveeta cheese
4 or 5 scallions, chopped
¼ cup green olives, chopped
½ cup Miracle Whip

Boil potatoes until done (about 20 minutes or until a fork pierces easily) while you cook the bacon in another pan till crisp. Drain both. Cut up cheese and potatoes; add the scallions and olives and mix all with Miracle Whip. (I know some folks think Miracle Whip is country, and perhaps it is, but that other kind of mayonnaise doesn't have the same tangy flavor). Crumble the bacon over the top and bake at 350 degrees in a greased 8 ½ by 11-inch glass pan for 25 to 30 minutes.

MAMA'S GERMAN FRIED POTATOES

Mama was Irish as Paddy's pig; she said 'me' for 'my,' but this was Papa's favorite way for her to fix potatoes, even if it was German.

3 or 4 good sized potatoes
Butter or bacon grease for frying
1 large onion, peeled and sliced
Paprika (sshhh)
Salt and pepper to taste

Cover the well scrubbed potatoes (You could peel them if you've a mind to, but I often don't. Just be sure to scrub 'em good first). Boil until they feel a bit soft when you press with the side of a spoon. About 20 minutes or so, depending on the size of the potatoes. Pour off the water and let them cool a few minutes. You can do this earlier in the day or the day before. Slice the potatoes into ¼ inch slices. Heat up a knob of butter or whatever you're using for fat—could use vegetable oil. Fry the onions for a little while till they're soft. Then add the potatoes, lifting them up and turning over with a spatula from time to time.

Don't tell anyone, but I sprinkle on some paprika as I turn them. Makes 'em look browned nicer. Cook all till nicely browned, even if artificially. Salt and pepper.

Papa liked these with fried eggs in the morning, but you can serve them later in the day if you want. As Andy Griffith says, "Gooooo—oood!"

GOLDIE'S POTATOES

It is sultry this morning and think rain is in the offing. I will have to get out my cooking vessels, as my roof leaks something fearful. Have pointed this out to my landlady. She is well-meaning but ineffectual. Can't get her husband to do anything about it. However, in the matter of cooking, we can now eat whether someone dies or not for Bill severed his connection with the buryin' ground. He is painting with Frank now. Makes more money and better working conditions. When he gets home from work, I'm going to make these potatoes, which I've named after myself.

4-5 medium potatoes
2 tablespoons butter
1 small sweet onion chopped.
¼ cup chopped mango (green bell pepper)
2 tablespoons flour
½ cup beef broth
Salt and pepper to taste
1 tablespoon chopped parsley

Peel and cut potatoes into chunks. Boil until done and drain and cool. In small pan or skillet, melt butter and cook onions and peppers until tender. Whisk in flour. Make sure flour is blended, no lumps, and whisk in broth. Slice potatoes to about ½ in and add to mixture. Add salt and pepper and parsley and simmer until gravy is thick.

COLCANNON

Mama's parents were born in Ireland—County Cork, I do believe. Her father was killed when a tree fell on him when she was but 6 years old. She then went to work with her mother as a seam over-caster. Then her mother died when she was 12 and she went to live with relatives. She recreated a dish she remembered her mother making, that she called "colcannon." She said it was for a holiday, but she didn't remember which one. Maybe you could look it up.*

2 or 3 large russet potatoes
Medium head of cabbage
1 large onion
½ cup milk
1 tablespoon butter
A small chunk of cheese, grated
Salt and pepper to taste

Peel the potatoes, cut into chunks and boil in lightly salted water till very tender. While the potatoes are cooking, finely chop the cabbage and onion. With a slotted spoon, lift the potatoes out of the water and set aside in a bowl while you cook the cabbage in the potato water. While they are cooking (about 5 minutes) mash the potatoes with the milk and butter till they're smooth. Add the onion and cabbage mixture to the potatoes and mix together with about 2/3 of the cheese. Transfer to a baking dish and sprinkle the rest of the cheese on top. Bake in a 350 oven for 15 or 20 minutes till all is warm and the cheese is slightly brown on top.

*Halloween

POTATO - CORN PUFFS

One vegetable I do love, is corn (which means it's probably not good for you). I use it often, so I have plenty on hand. I'm so thankful that we now have freezers so that I can freeze corn on the cob. Your grandfather doesn't always like to use his teeth. Mostly, they're in a glass in the bathroom or in his shirt pocket. But, if I cut the corn off the cob, he has no trouble and he loves it almost as well as I do. I also, being the frugal lady that I am, use most leftovers. This is one thing I do with leftover mashed potatoes and corn.

1 cup mashed potatoes
1 cup corn (fresh or canned or even frozen)
2 well beaten eggs
3 tablespoons milk
1 teaspoon chopped parsley
1 teaspoon baking powder
½ cup flour
Salt and pepper to taste
Oil enough for deep frying

Mix all ingredients together to form a batter. It should be loose enough to drop from a spoon. Drop by teaspoon into hot oil and cook until brown. Drain on towels. All in all, a very nice side dish.

NED'S LIMA BEANS

Columbus Day, 1962

My Dear

I've had three faulty vertebrae since birth and have been having a problem with my back lately, so went to the Bluffton Clinic and afterward spent a week in a nursing home recuperating. They put me in with two roommates, one 88 and the other 91. I felt like a mere child. The day I went in, Ollie, the 88-year-old nodded toward Julia and said in a conspiratorial voice, "She's nuts." She hesitated a moment and with a roguish smile added, "I'm half nuts." Then from the room next door you never heard such a cacophony—the inmate, who was rather deaf had two visitors who roared at her rather than talked. It was funny but mostly you smiled with a lump in your throat.

They served us some rather nasty lima beans. Had they asked I'd have given them this recipe that Ned served us when we were out in California.

1 small onion, chopped
1 mango chopped (bell pepper)
2 tablespoons butter
2 cups cooked, diced tomatoes
2 cups baby lima beans
Salt and pepper to taste
1 teaspoon Worcestershire sauce
1 ½ cups grated cheese (I like American cheese)

Cook the onion and mango in butter until tender. Add tomatoes and simmer for about 10 minutes. Drain lima beans and add beans, salt, pepper and Worcestershire sauce. Cook together for about 20 minutes. In a greased casserole dish, alternate layers of beans and cheese and bake in 350-degree oven for about 30 minutes. I sometimes like to add some diced ham to this and make it a one-dish meal.

BEAUTY INSURANCE BROCCOLI BAKE

I took out some medical insurance the other day and on the back of my application he wrote, "She is past 80 but looks 60." I had already signed the application, so it wasn't bribery. I figure it's 'cause I eat so many vegetables. This is a good one to get people to eat when they say they don't like veggies.

3 stalks broccoli
1 beaten egg
1 can cream of mushroom soup

1 cup grated cheddar cheese
¼ cup milk
1 tablespoon finely chopped onion
2 tablespoon melted butter
½ cup breadcrumbs

Cut broccoli into small pieces and steam in a bit of water till it's bright green. Don't cook it too long or it tastes sulphurous. Put in baking dish. Mix egg, soup, cheese, milk, and onion and pour over the broccoli. Mix butter and breadcrumbs and spread over broccoli. Bake at 350 for 45 minutes, uncovered.

LITTLE NELL'S CANDIED CARROTS

I saw your high school English teacher the other day and she said to remember you to her, or her to you, whichever. Said you had been one of her favorite English students. Do you remember when your friend Jane came up to the lake and said she'd written a book report for Mrs. S's class on the Olde Curiosity Shoppe, which is among my favorites? I was rather nonplussed when she confessed she didn't know Little Nell had died, since that is a pivotal scene in the book. She admitted she had not read all of the book! Wanted to mention to Joanne, that Little Nell had died but thought it might not be polite to do so.

Jane also said she didn't care much for vegetables, but when I made these while she was there, she gobbled them up with gusto.

6 medium carrots
½ cup water

1 cup brown sugar
4 tablespoon butter

Clean and cut carrots in strips as you would for carrot sticks. In a baking dish, mix water, sugar and butter and warm, mixing to make a syrup-like mixture. Add carrots and make sure they're covered with syrup. Bake at 350 degrees about 20 minutes.

Ed. Note: This is another book by Charles Dickens. When Grandmother and her future sister-in-law Jess went to California, they went to the theater and saw the play, "The Olde Curiosity Shoppe." She loved to tell the story about a woman during the play who became so caught up in Little Nell's death scene that she screamed out, "Oh My Lord, won't somebody please help that poor child!"

HAIRY CHESTED CABBAGE

When I was a little girl, I used to hate cooked cabbage. Papa told me it would put hair on my chest. I was pretty sure that I didn't want that. I did, however grow to love cabbage in any form, cooked or otherwise. So far, no hair there. I never doubted Papa, but he used to love to tease me.

1 medium sized head of cabbage
2 well beaten eggs
1 tablespoon melted butter
3 tablespoons cream
Salt and pepper to taste

Heat oven to 325. Clean and quarter cabbage. Cook in boiling water for 15 minutes. Drain and let cool. When cooled, chop very fine and add eggs, butter, cream, salt and pepper. Put into buttered baking dish and bake for 30 minutes

IRRATIONALLY PICKLED BEETS

I have been so uncommonly healthy lately that I've been feeling I should do something irrational. So, I went out and trimmed the two spirea bushes on either side of the front walk. Call me madcap! I had enough energy left over to do something else, so I made Bill's favorite pickled beets.

4 cups sliced cooked beets
1 large sweet onion
2 cups vinegar
1 teaspoon salt
Dash pepper
1 teaspoon brown sugar
1 teaspoon caraway seeds

Slice beets (you can used canned, though fresh are better) and onions to about 1/8 Thick. Combine with other ingredients and bring to a boil. Lower heat to simmer for about 3 minutes. Put beets and onions in sterilized jars and pour in vinegar mixture to the top. Let stand for 24 hours before using. This will make about 3 pints.

When a few of the beets are used in the jar, I make pickled eggs. I just add peeled, hard-boiled eggs to the jar. They color up so beautifully that they're lovely to look at and quite scrumptious to boot.

COMPANY BAKED STUFFED TOMATOES

I love cooking for company, and they don't seem to complain. At least the plates are clean when they get up from the table. Had Thelma, Edna and Ethel over I made stuffed tomatoes for us. It's a fairly light lunch and mighty good! There I go again, blowing my own horn. I guess I toot it just in case no one else does.

4-6 medium sized tomatoes
1 ½ cups bread or cracker crumbs
1 tablespoon minced onion
1 egg beaten
2 tablespoons melted butter
1 teaspoon chopped parsley
Salt and pepper to taste

Cut out centers of cleaned tomatoes. Chop the tomato centers and combine with the other ingredients and fill the tomato shells. Put into a baking dish and bake at 350 degrees for about 30 minutes. I usually add some grated cheese just after I take it out of the oven. Any kind of cheese will do but I love American.

CLOSE HARMONY SLAW

The Gaither clan has formed a trio and are becoming well known in the Christian music circles. They sound quite love-ly. I remember when Mary Jo got married and you played the organ for Billy Jim to sing. You later told me that he and you girls and a couple of other young men had driven around Alec that night, singing in harmony. That sounds like it might have been fun, but I would hope the driver had given his entire attention to the road. Can't think how he would have.

Kane was over the other evening to watch them on television and brought this as her contribution. It was so good we had some bread and butter with it and called it dinner. Mostly because my contribution was apple dumplings and we wanted to save room for them.

1 head cabbage
½ cup vegetable oil
2 tablespoons apple cider vinegar
½ teaspoons mustard
¼ teaspoons celery salt
2 Tablespoons Miracle Whip
Salt and pepper
Paprika

Chop the cabbage and put in a bowl. In another small bowl, mix oil and vinegar. Add the mustard—the kind in a jar, not the powdered kind—celery salt, Miracle Whip, salt and pepper to taste and paprika. Mix it up and pour over the cabbage, then mix that up. This is best made far enough ahead for the flavors to blend. You can cut this in half if there are not a lot to eat it. It does make quite a large bowlful, though it keeps in the icebox for several days if you cover it.

HISTORICAL CAULIFLOWER WITH CHEESE SAUCE

Lee is coming home in March and so is Jack for two weeks. What would make that picture complete, now that Sue and her progeny are here, would be a visit from you and yours. I surely hope it comes true; I love you all so dearly. Sue and I are making amazing strides on our family history. When they were down here last Sunday, I did the usual chicken baked in the oven with butter and Rice Krispies for dinner. I also had cauliflower with cheese sauce. I'm pretty sure you know how to make cauliflower, but not so sure about the cheese sauce, so here they both are.

1 medium head cauliflower
3 tablespoons butter
3 tablespoons flour
½ teaspoon salt
Pepper to taste
1 ½ cups milk
1 cup grated sharp cheese (cheddar)

Break the cauliflower into flowerets and if they're too big, cut those in half. Put in pan with small amount of water, cover pan and bring the water to a boil. Turn heat down and simmer for about 5 minutes or until the vegetable is to your liking. I like mine to be what you'd consider overcooked, but you may like yours a bit less soft.

Meanwhile, in another small pan, melt butter and remove from heat. Stir in flour, salt and pepper. Very gradually add the milk, stirring constantly until thick and smooth. Cook over low heat for about 5 minutes more and add cheese, stirring until well blended. Pour over cauliflower in a serving dish.

If you serve this with my ubiquitous RK chicken, you can pretend you're sitting here with us.

SQUAW CORN

Aug. 28, 1962

My Dears

So glad to hear from you. I am completely senile, I guess. I didn't cry when either of you girls went back to California and now every time I think of either of you—and that is frequently—I pucker up. I am not given to bawling as a general thing, but when your mother left Sunday evening, I had to fight back tears. My neighbor, Mae came across the street and stayed till 9:00 PM, which helped considerably, although I did miss Mr. Ed.

She was so nice to stay, and we had a lovely visit over a supper of what Papa called Squaw Corn. You can use canned or frozen corn if fresh is out of season. I happened also to have some fresh tomatoes and we had those with it. I know how you pine for Indiana tomatoes, which I can't supply, but you can do the corn if you've a mind to.

8 Slices of Bacon
3 Small onions sliced thin
Fresh corn cut from about 8 ears
½ teaspoons salt
8 eggs, beaten
8 slices of toast

Cut bacon into little pieces and fry in skillet. Add onions and cook until brown. Add corn and salt and continue to cook until corn is also browned. Add beaten eggs and cook until thickened, keep stirring, scraping the bottom of the skillet. Serve over toast.

Mary Goldie Montgomery
Circa 1912. Age 28

Mary G. Jolliff
Circa 1943. Age 59

Grandmother, Granddaddy and Jeco at Lake cottage. Circa 1952

All-purpose stove at the cottage.

Mary Goldie Montgomery
Circa. 1910. Age 26

MAIN DISHES

MOTHER HUBBARD CORNMEAL CASSEROLE

Spring has pretty nearly come. The trees are beginning to bud and the birds are all back and I'm glad I didn't die this winter. I needed to fix something for our supper this evening and the cupboard was alarmingly bare, or nearly so. Fortunately, there was a hunk of cheese that Bill hadn't eaten so I thought I'd use up some cornmeal I also found. I do know that you don't fancy meat and frankly, I can't abide much myself so when I came across this recipe on the back of something or other, I thought of you.

½ cup corn meal
2 ½ cups boiling water
½ pound grated cheddar cheese
½ cup milk
½ teaspoon salt
Paprika

Set oven to 350 degrees. Make a mush by adding corn meal gradually to boiling salted water. Make sure you stir constantly. Cook for about 30 minutes, stirring fairly often. Pour into a shallow pan and chill. When cold, cut into 1-in squares. Melt the cheese over double boiler. Add milk gradually and remember to stir constantly. Alternate layers of mush and cheese in a casserole dish and bake for 20 minutes. Sprinkle with paprika and it's ready to serve. *Pretty easy and very good.*

VEGETABLE UPSIDE-DOWN CAKE

My old crony, Katy just called me with the exciting news that she just got a new washer. I'm glad I didn't, for I'd feel obliged to use it if I did. She also told me the most wonderful way to use up leftover vegetables. At first, I think I didn't pay attention to the veggie part and imagined it would be a sweet, fruity dessert, but I was pleasantly surprised at how this turned out. It only occurred to me later that I could do the same thing with Bisquick in place of the flour, baking powder and butter. You could too if you're as lazy as I am.

2 cups flour
2 teaspoons baking powder
¼ cup + 2 tablespoons butter
1 egg beaten
1 cup milk
Salt and pepper to taste
½ chopped onion
4 cups cooked vegetables (carrots, peas, green beans, etc.)
½ cup vegetable or chicken stock
Tomato sauce

Mix and sift the dry ingredients. Cut in ¼ cup of butter. Combine the egg and milk and add to the dry ingredients. Stir until it's mixed well. Season the vegetables with the salt and pepper and put them into a baking pan. Add the vegetable stock and dot with the 2 tablespoons of butter. Spread the dough mixture over the top of the vegetables.

Bake in a hot oven at 425 degrees for about 25 to 30 minutes. Turn out onto a hot serving plate with the vegetables on the top. I like to top mine with tomato sauce or sometimes, a little mushroom sauce.

TOMATO SAUCE

2 teaspoons butter
1 diced onion
2 tablespoons flour
1 ½ cups strained cooked tomatoes
Salt and pepper to taste

Melt butter and add onion. Cook until tender. Add flour and mix well. Add the tomatoes gradually, stirring constantly so as not to burn on the bottom of the pan. Boil for about 5 minutes and add salt and pepper.

SPINACH & CHEESE GOBLIN CASSEROLE

Keri Jo says, and I quote, "There is no sucha thing as goblins." She admits there are fairies, but no goblins. I told her they had never seen them because they had been so good, but Craig said, "I don't say my prayers." Kids are just too smart for great-grandmothers. He also 'lowed he didn't like vegetables. I made this for them, and he suspicioned it might've had vegetables in it, but he ate it right up anyway.

2 10-ounce packages frozen spinach, thawed
1/3 cup grated cheese
2 cups cottage cheese
2 eggs, beaten
1 teaspoon salt

Drain and press the water from the spinach. Mix all ingredients until well blended and transfer to a baking dish. Bake at 350 for 30 minutes. What could be easier?

LEAKY ROOF CORN PUDDING

I got mad at my landlord because he won't fix my screen or my kitchen ceiling, so I am ready to move out. I found another place that I like, but the rent is a bit steep--$21 a week. That cuts deeply into my monthly allotment. Am thinking of taking in wash, but that would be a bit of a problem, as I have neither a washer nor a clothesline to hang it on. Neither do I have a car nor driver to take me to the laundromat. So, I guess it's a bad idea. I always hated to iron anyway so I need to write a bestseller.

I will be so glad when Sue gets here. She is another of my favorite granddaughters. She always liked this corn pudding and will make it for her when she arrives.

3 eggs
1 (14 ounce) can corn
2 tablespoon melted butter
2 cups milk
1 teaspoon salt
1/8 teaspoon pepper
½ teaspoon sugar
Cracker crumbs
Butter

Beat eggs well. Combine with corn, melted butter and milk. Stir well. Add seasoning and sugar. Pour into well-buttered casserole dish. Sprinkle with cracker crumbs, dot with butter and bake in 350-degree oven for about 40 minutes. This was enough for about 5 or 6 people.

INDIANA SOUL FOOD
(Green beans, potatoes and ham)

Honey, I know you modern young women like to leave your vegetables almost raw, but I still cook 'em till they can't bite back, like Mama did.

Thick slice ham—about ¼ to ½ pound
Medium onion
3 or 4 garlic cloves or garlic powder.
1 ½ pound fresh green beans
3 or 4 nice size potatoes
Salt and pepper

Cut ham up into about 1-inch cubes. Peel and chop the onion. Also the garlic cloves if using, or sprinkle garlic powder when all assembled. Stem the beans and break into a couple or three pieces. This is one place where I do peel the potatoes, and cut them into ¾ inch cubes. Put all in a large kettle with water to just barely cover. Heat to boiling and then simmer for a couple of hours. Serve with homemade bread or cornbread. This'll make you homesick.

DOWN UNDER GOULASH

Sept 30, 1965

My Dear,

Another nasty, cold, rainy day. I am tired of them, as we have had an overdose of them lately. I've been sleeping under my electric blanket, which is ridiculous this early in the season.

I suppose you are flying around in circles to get ready to leave for Australia, though I can hardly see you in that role. You're not really a flyer arounder. In fact, as you know, you've always been a bit glaikit, but somehow you manage to do things. I'd dearly love to see the babies before you go. Also, their mom, but I do think this would be slightly (some 6,000 miles) out of your way. But I'll be glad when Jean gets home.

I'm going to make Bill some goulash, which he loves, for his dinner if I can mooch an onion off Mary Jo. I have everything else. Wonder if they eat such peasant fare Down Under?

1 box elbow macaroni
1 pound ground beef
1 small onion diced
1 (14 ounce) can diced tomatoes
1 (14 ounce can tomato sauce
Salt and pepper to taste
Grated cheddar cheese

Boil macaroni in salted water until tender. Fry ground beef, crumbling as you fry. Add diced onion and cook until the onion is clear colored. Add tomatoes and sauce and salt and pepper. Add cooked macaroni and let simmer for about 10-15 minutes to let flavors blend. Remove from heat and top with grated cheese to serve.

I love you all a bushel and a peck and much, much more. Kiss the babies for me.

Ganu

MORE'S THE PITY CORNED BEEF HASH & EGGS

Wayne went to Lodge last night and Ethel came in and stayed with me until 10:30. She usually goes to Bessie's, but Bessie has company right now and they planned a thrilling game of dominoes. Ethel wasn't sure she could bear the excitement, so she came here, instead. I felt sort of like Mother Hubbard when I surveyed the contents of my cupboard and was slightly embarrassed by what I gave her for supper, but she announced that it just hit the spot. Here it is if you find yourself in a similar position and no way to get to the store:

1 (14 ounce) can Hormel's corned beef hash
3 or 4 eggs
A bit of cooking oil
Salt & pepper

Put the can in the icebox for a bit, as that firms it up for slicing. Open at both ends and slide out. Cut into 3 or 4 slices. Put a film of oil in a skillet and brown the slices on one side over medium heat—about 3 or 4 minutes. Turn over and turn the heat down slightly. Use a spoon and make a depression in each slice, into which you carefully break an egg—one each slice. Salt and pepper and cover the skillet. Cook for another 3 or 4 minutes or until the yolks are to your liking and serve.

Some people like to have toast with it, but we didn't, as we are neither particularly large eaters.

MEAT PIE

Although beef was never my cup of tea (neither is tea for that matter) your grandfather seems to like it so I make it for him. Also, for company when we have it. Seems to go over well either way.

½ medium yellow onion diced
2 tablespoons butter
2 tablespoons flour
1 ½ cups beef broth
1 tablespoon Worcestershire Sauce
About 2 cups cooked, diced beef
(left over pot roast or new is fine)
1 cup sliced cooked carrots
1 cup cooked peas
1 cup diced cooked potatoes
Salt and pepper to taste

Baking powder biscuits either from the rolled package or off the Bisquick box. Or make your own from scratch (p. 19). Cook onions in butter until tender. Add flour and whisk in until mixed. Add beef broth and Worcestershire Sauce and whisk in, making a thin gravy. Add beef, carrots, potatoes and peas. I add salt and pepper and taste. Pour mixture into a buttered baking dish. Place biscuits on top of mixture and put into hot (425 degrees) oven. Bake until biscuits are golden brown. About 15 to 20 minutes.

ROAST CHICKEN

I am told, though haven't personally read it, that there is a recipe that begins, "First catch your hare." That sounds pretty basic to me as it is actually what we did with chickens. I was always too "chicken hearted" to kill them though, so Mama never made me do it. There are some modern things I'm thoroughly grateful for, and buying an already killed, cleaned chicken is one of them. I could never abide the stench of burned feathers that arose when we singed the pin feathers.

The way I roast a chicken is not how most folks do it, but since I need the broth for noodles, I always boil the chicken—actually simmer it—first for about a half hour for the broth. You could dispense with that part if you're not making noodles or dumplings, though why anybody wouldn't is beyond my powers of comprehension.

So, get an aged, good-sized hen and put in a kettle you haven't burned up, barely cover with water and bring to a boil. I usually add an onion, halved, not peeled and some chopped celery and grated carrots. Skim off the scum that rises and turn the heat to simmer. After a half hour, remove the chicken to a baking pan and pour melted butter all over. They are sometimes kind of dry after being boiled. Place in pre-heated 350-degree oven for another half hour or a bit more, till browned and the leg moves easily. Baste with more butter from time to time. Add the resultant juices to the broth and cook your previously made noodles or dumplings in it.

MAMA'S DUMPLINGS

I haven't written for longer than I meant. I've been a little under the weather, which I also didn't mean to. Out of my control, I fear. I am better now and felt like writing at least. I don't feel like cleaning the house but that has nothing to do with my condition. I never feel much like cleaning. Most people believe that all women should be good housekeepers. I always felt that was like saying all men should be good carpenters.

My niece Edna and her husband Fred stopped to visit. It was good to see them. I put on a meager fare for dinner, but they seemed to like it. I had made chicken and dumplings and had leftovers. They didn't stay much after dinner, but we had a good visit, nonetheless. You had said that you couldn't make dumplings so am telling you the way Mama taught me.

2 cup flour
1 ¼ teaspoons baking powder
Dash salt
1 tablespoon butter or some fat (Of course, Mama used lard)
About 2/3 cup milk

Sift flour, baking powder and salt together. Add butter and work in with fork. Add sufficient milk and make a soft dough. Turn out onto a well-floured board and roll out to about ½ in thick. Cut into small squares. Drop into hot liquid, probably chicken broth. Cover and cook for about 25 minutes. This should make about 12 dumplings or so. Make sure that it's well covered.

REAL FRIED CHICKEN

October 12, 1961

My Dearest One,

Have been missing you all so dreadfully and now with the arrival of my great-grandson, I believe I will come for a visit. The Greyhound has a package deal—two go for $62.50 each and stay 45 days and then they fetch you home by any scenic route you choose—FREE! The trouble at the moment is, that I cannot find a second one to go with, and anyway, I don't think I want to come back as early as 45 days.

Or I could go by Trailways. I'm not up to carrying much and with them I could get on the bus at Indianapolis and not have to change, so wouldn't have to lug my luggage. It takes 49 hours from Indianapolis to L.A. You can have your meals served if you wish, but I would not wish. I like to get off the bus and probably would not like what they served in any case. I eat pretty light when I travel.

When you girls and your mother took the train down to join your dad in Miami that year just after the war began, I sent along a big box of fried chicken. Here's how I made it.

1 tablespoon seasoned salt
1 tablespoon pepper
½ cup flour
1 (3 pound) chicken in serving pieces
Cooking oil

In paper lunch bag, combine seasoned salt, pepper and flour. Add chicken, a few pieces at a time, and toss to coat. In a deep, 12-inch skillet,

74

heat 1-inch oil over medium-high heat and cook chicken, turning twice, 25 minutes or until chicken is thoroughly cooked; drain on paper towels.

Okay, I'm going to confess to you that I used bacon grease instead of oil. This was in the days before cholesterol was invented. There was also no sucha thing as Lawry's seasoned salt at that time either, but I became rather attached to it when you introduced me to it and now use it for this.

TANGY CHICKEN 57

They had chickens on sale at the Thriftway for 19 cents a pound and I called and ordered one that looks like a young turkey and it was 66 cents total! However, we are just about all chickened out, as we eat it a lot since it's cheap. I try to fix it in as many different ways as possible to disguise it, but it doesn't work. I can always recognize it. Here's an easy one that all seem to like a lot.

2 to 2 ½ pound chicken pieces
2 tablespoons butter
½ cup Heinz 57 Sauce
½ cup water

Brown chicken in skillet in the butter. Combine ½ cup (or more if you want more sauce) Heinz 57 Sauce and water and pour over the chicken. Cover and simmer 30 to 40 minutes till tender, basting occasionally. Skim the excess fat—or you could start with skinless. Spoon the sauce over the chicken and serve over rice or noodles.

This one's a bit too tangy for me, but everyone else loves it.

KRISPIE OVEN-FRIED CHICKEN

Sometimes when I'm feeling too lazy to actually fry a chicken, I do this. I think I found the recipe in a Woman's Day or one of those magazines your mother brings me from the beauty shop.

Cut-up fryer (2 to 2/12 lbs)
Half a cube of melted oleo (or butter if you're feeling flush)
Salt and pepper
2 cups Rice Krispies

Dip the chicken pieces in melted butter. Salt and pepper to taste. Pulverize the krispies and roll the chicken in them. Place on a cookie sheet and bake in a 350 oven 30 minutes, or until tender. Beats fried chicken. Well, almost.

Gravy:
You can also make wonderful gravy, too. Just take a pancake turner and scrape up the residue and put in a deeper vessel and make in usual gravy fashion. That is, add in a bit more butter—maybe a tablespoon, and add a couple of tablespoons of flour. Cook over medium heat till golden brown and then slowly add milk or leftover potato water or whatever, stirring the while. It'll make lovely gravy. I sprinkle a handful of ground up Rice Krispies lot of things—like potato soup, scalloped potatoes and always in gravy.

CHICKEN N' NOODLES

I am having Zelma over today for dinner. She's a good old scout and is helpful to me, sometimes even washing my sheets when I can't get to the laundromat. Bill will be painting and it's not handy for him to come home midday. I made him a sandwich—well actually two, as he is a growing boy of 51—which he will eat during a break. I also included a rather heroic slice of peach pie. I thought I'd make old-fashioned chicken and noodles for Zelma and me and then I can heat it up for supper this evening and have it again.

Chicken
1 (2 to 3 pound) chicken cut in pieces
4 stalks diced celery with tops
1 grated carrot
1 onion, halved—unpeeled
Black pepper to taste
3 (14 ounce) cans chicken broth

Noodles
4 cups flour
1 teaspoon salt
3 eggs
1 tablespoon vegetable oil

Chicken
In a large pot over medium heat, combine chicken, celery and their tops, carrot, onion and its peel, and pepper. Pour broth over and bring to a boil. Cover, reduce heat and simmer until chicken is tender and falls from the bone, about 45 minutes.

Noodles While chicken is cooking, make noodles. Place the flour and salt in a large bowl and make a well in the center into which you put the eggs and oil. Begin beating the eggs with a fork, incorporating flour as you go. (Some people use only egg yolks. If you do that double the number. Use the whites for meringue on a pie.) When it starts to be hard to work with—Mama used to say, "When it feels right"—turn it out to a floured board and begin to knead it for a few minutes, adding flour if it starts to be too sticky. Then cover it and let it rest a bit. Twenty minutes or so.

Then cut the dough into 4 sections and roll each one thin, sprinkle with a little flour and roll it up like a jelly roll. With a sharp knife, begin with the rolled edge toward you and slice the roll into about 1 quarter inch noodles, wider if you like. When you unroll them, you can cut them shorter if you want. Put that batch to dry on a clean tea towel and do the other three. Sometimes I make the noodles the day before, as it's time consuming.

Chicken again Now back to the chicken which will have cooled some. Strain chicken stock, reserving meat, celery and carrots. Pull meat from bones, get rid of the skin and return strained stock and meat, celery and carrots to pot.

Chicken n' noodles Bring to a boil and drop the noodles into the pot by handfuls. Let them boil for a couple of minutes and take off the stove. Let it sit for a bit and then it's ready to serve.

That's actually a recipe for when you are flush. When we were poor as Job's Turkey during the Depression, we made this with chicken backs and necks. It was still good, but not so meaty as this version.

CHICKEN N' NOODLES AND MASHED POTATOES

We often have this over mashed potatoes, which I know sounds very starchy, but is so delicious you won't care. Just glop the potatoes (p. 43) on the plate and make a hollow in the middle into which you ladle a generous helping of the noodles. Ummm-good!

BILL'S CHICKEN-FRIED STEAK N' GRAVY

Your Uncle Bill always likes this for his dinner. I guess you call it lunch out there. Nowadays when you invite someone to eat dinner you have to specify whether you mean midday or evening. Bill eats this in the daytime.

Cube steaks—one for each person
Salt and pepper
Garlic powder
3 tablespoons flour plus more for dredging
Bacon grease or butter for frying
2 to 2 ½ cups milk

Salt and pepper both sides of steaks. Sprinkle with garlic powder. Put flour in a plate and dredge the steaks in it. Now pound in the flour. If you don't have one of those meat tenderizers, you can use the edge of a saucer. Repeat with all the steaks.

Put a glob of bacon grease or butter in a frying pan and heat till sizzling. I know you want to watch your weight but you gotta use fat to brown these properly. Also for the gravy. Fry the steaks for 1 to 2 minutes a side or until golden brown. Remove to a warm plate and place in a warm oven while you make the gravy.

Sprinkle 3 tablespoons flour in the pan and scrape up the brown goodies as you stir till it's mixed and sort of golden. Pour in milk little by little, stirring the while until it thickens. You might not have to use all the milk. Pour over the steak.

If there's any gravy leftover and I didn't make potatoes, Bill puts gravy over bread and finishes it up. He shouldn't, for he's getting to be a right jolly old elf, tubby as Santa, himself.

POINT TAVERN BAKED HAM

I have become a chef—a paid one! Jack has been tending bar at the Point Tavern Friday and Saturday night and they like to have a baked ham so they can sell sandwiches on weekends. Jack 'lowed as how I make a pretty nifty baked ham, so I got elected to provide it. He says the customers rave about it and it brings them in by droves. I'm sure it's the ham and not the beer, which is available all week.

15 lb Ham (bone in)
whole cloves
1 large (14 ounce) can pineapple chunks
Pineapple juice from can
½ cup brown sugar
1 tablespoon yellow mustard

Place ham into large baking pan with plenty of foil under for wrapping. Wrap ham and put into 325-degree oven for about 3 ½ hours. Remove from oven and unwrap ham. Score the ham with a sharp knife into a diamond pattern. Stick a clove in each intersection of the points of the diamonds. Also using toothpicks, put pineapple chunks on each diamond.

In a separate bowl, mix the brown sugar, mustard and pineapple juice and pour mixture over ham. Place back into the oven for another hour, basting with the pan drippings every 15 minutes or so. When done, remove toothpicks and cloves for serving.

SIMMERED SPICED HAM

Here's another way I used to make ham. I think it's pretty tasty, although not so popular as the ham I make for the Point. Maybe it's not as nice a visual presentation, though it's hard to envision the denizens of the Point as appreciators of artistic endeavors.

1 (12-15 pound) ham
Dash ground cinnamon
Dash ground cloves
Dash Allspice
2 small onions
1 cup breadcrumbs
1 cup brown sugar
1 ½ cups grape juice

Cover ham with water and add the cinnamon, cloves, allspice and onions. Simmer over low heat, for about 20 minutes per pound. Drain. Remove the skin and cut the fat in a criss-cross pattern. Place ham in a roasting pan, cover with mixture of breadcrumbs and brown sugar. Pour the grape juice into the pan. Bake in a slow oven at 300 degrees for about 10 minutes per pound. Baste occasionally with juice. You'll love the flavor of the ham with the grape juice.

MAMA'S HAM CASSEROLE

My Dears:

A bit nippy today so I'll do something different and stay home. I normally do that anyway but good to have an excuse. I hope you got the information regarding our family tree. Most of the branches are sturdy although some not so much. All in all, a good lot. Mama used to love for the family to be together and would have such a feast when she could. She was a pretty good cook. At least most plates were clean at dinner's end.

One thing she loved to make was a ham casserole. I loved it. I'll include the recipe to the best of my recollection. Mama didn't have a set recipe and she taught me to cook in the same manner. I don't remember Mama having a set of measuring spoons as many do now, nor did she have a measuring cup. Her eye did just fine. She'd say, "That looks about right." And it was.

1 cup cooked chopped ham
1 tablespoon cooking oil
1 small onion, chopped
4 eggs
Salt and Pepper to taste
½ cup milk
1 cup diced potatoes
¼ cup chopped parsley

Chop cooked ham into small bite sized pieces. Into skillet, using cooking oil, add ham and onions. Cook with a low flame until the onions are fairly cooked. Beat eggs and add salt, pepper and milk. Combine all ingredients and put into oven at 350 degrees. Cook about 45 minutes or until the eggs begin to brown and it puffs nicely.

INDIANA HAM AND BEANS

I have put some beans to soak and was checking my watch to see when my programs begin when I thought of something that happened when Harry was about seven or so. Perry always carried a pocket watch and one day Harry asked him the time. Perry responded that he didn't know and couldn't find out as he'd used up all his looks for the day. Harry, a bit puzzled, asked him to explain, so Perry told him that when a watchmaker takes the back off a watch to fix it, there's a long number on the back called a serial number. This number represents the number of looks you can take at a timepiece, after which it dies. So, you have to ration the number of looks you take at a watch. Harry was not entirely convinced but wasn't sure where the hole was in such logic.

While you're mulling that one over, here's the recipe for good ole' Indiana ham and beans to go with cornbread.

1 pound white navy beans
1 pound cooked ham cut in bite-sized pieces.
    (you can used ham hocks)
Salt and pepper to taste
½ cup chopped onions (optional)

Soak beans overnight in large pot filled with enough water to cover beans. Rinse and drain beans. Put beans and ham into large pot with a little more than enough water to cover and bring to a boil. As soon as the water begins to boil, cut the heat and let simmer for about an hour or until the beans are tender. Take care not to let the liquid steam away. Add salt and pepper sparingly as the ham will be salty. If you've used ham hocks, take them out, cut away the fat and return the meat to the beans.

Your granddad and I liked to put raw chopped onion on top to serve. I also like to serve them over cornbread. A lot of folks in Indiana also make fried potatoes with this, but I always thought this was sufficient by itself, so never did.

ADAM'S FAMOUS BARBECUED RIBS

I went over to Elwood the day after Christmas and Rosemary and Adam took numerous pictures. Rosemary brought some of them over and in two of them I was showing my behind. I mean literally! Adam had insisted on my taking a drink with him to show him I liked him. I'll bet that was why I was so abandoned. I was wearing underpants, though, you'll be relieved to know.

He had made his 'famous' barbecued ribs, which were a bit too tangy for my taste but there was considerable lip smacking done in other quarters, so I deduced that they were more than edible. Adam was so proud of his 'secret' recipe that he couldn't help himself and shared it with me, perhaps due to his own abandoned state. Now you have the secret.

2 pounds spareribs (beef or pork)
1 medium onion
1 tablespoon cooking oil
1 tablespoon Worcestershire sauce
¼ cup lemon juice
2 tablespoons brown sugar
2 tablespoons vinegar
½ cup water
Salt & pepper
1 cup chili sauce

Cut ribs into serving portions and place in baking pan. Bake for 30 minutes at 350 degrees. Meantime chop the onion and brown it in the oil. Then add all the other ingredients and simmer for 20 minutes. Take the ribs out of the oven and pour off all the rendered fat. Pour the sauce over the ribs and bake for another hour. Or, you could turn the oven down and slow-bake for several hours till you're ready to serve them.

PORK N' KRISPIES STEW

Last Sunday Bill went down and got my stuff for dinner—77 cents worth of pork cutlets (they are nearly as cheap as chicken and a nice alternative). I was expecting no one but Bill for dinner but your mother came down somewhat unexpectedly. She'd been the week before and I thought she had elsewhere to go, but she wanted to give me a permanent, as I've been looking a bit wild lately. She must've noticed. Here's what we had:

3 pork cutlets
1 medium onion
2 tablespoons butter
3 medium potatoes
½ small head cabbage
Salt & pepper to taste
1 cup crushed Rice Krispies
½ cup milk (or more)

Cut up the cutlets into about 1-inch pieces and brown in butter. Set aside and brown the chopped onion in the butter. Peel and cube the potatoes and chop the cabbage. You can also add carrots to this if you've a mind to. Transfer all to large kettle (I had to use the only one

I haven't burned up lately) and let stew over lowish heat until it is not so juicy—maybe half hour to 45 minutes or longer. Add Rice Krispies and milk. Salt and pepper to taste.

Yes, I know it sounds strange, but it is very tasty. Your mother ate it without comment. She is much like her taciturn father.

FRIED LAKE FISH

We don't eat a great deal of fish and I eat nearly none at all. Nevertheless, the last time Harry's were at the lake they brought me a mess of bass and perch—mercifully cleaned and beheaded—and I fried them up and they were quite tasty.

2 pounds or more of small fish
1 teaspoon salt
¼ cup flour or corn meal
½ cup vegetable oil.

Mix the salt with the flour or corn meal in a shallow dish and dredge each piece of fish in it. Lay the fish in hot fat and turn in 2 to 5 minutes or as soon as golden. Brown the other side and take up immediately after both sides are browned. Be careful not to overcook as it gets dry.

MAE'S FAVORITE SALMON PATTIES

The sun is shining to beat the band, but it is only 32 and cold as whiz. I'm ag'in it. Do so hate the cold. I am going on a cleaning spree today and it is about time. Glen gave me a Bissel Sweeper and it really takes up the dirt, but it has to be applied. Bill ran it everyday when he was home, but I have to do it now. Not my favorite activity, I fear. Then I think I'll make salmon patties for supper and maybe ask Mae over, as she has a weakness for them.

1 (14 ounce) can salmon
½ cup milk
2 eggs lightly beaten
2/3 cup breadcrumbs or rolled oats
½ teaspoon salt
½ small onion diced.
1 tablespoon Worcestershire sauce
Butter or cooking oil for frying

Mix all ingredients together except butter. Add breadcrumbs or oats slowly to gain the consistency to form patties. Place in hot skillet and fry until brown on both sides. Or you can place on an oiled cookie sheet, brush the patties with a bit of oil and bake at 350 degrees for 30 minutes.

DESSERTS

RHUBARB CRISP

Zelma from next door, (your mother went to school with her) has a sort of rag tag garden but it manages to grow a few things. Rhubarb among 'em. She brought me enough for Coxey's Army the other day. I couldn't possibly use it all, so when your Aunt Trevella came by yesterday I sent her home with a bunch. Your Uncle Harry is quite fond of rhubarb pie. I felt too lazy to make pie crust, so I made a crisp instead with what was left.

4 cups cut up rhubarb
Dash salt
1 1/3 to 2 cups of sugar
¾ cup flour
1 teaspoon cinnamon
½ cup butter (Don't use oleo—not as good).

Heat a medium oven (350 degrees) Put the rhubarb in a baking dish and sprinkle with the salt. Put sugar, flour and cinnamon into a bowl and add the butter, mixing thoroughly till crumbly. Sprinkle this over the rhubarb and bake 40 or 50 minutes. You can tell if it's done when the topping is golden brown.

There's them as likes this with ice cream and those who favor whipped cream. Either is good.

HELEN'S DATE PUDDING

I was able, by dint of friendly persuasion, to inveigle Helen into sharing her cherished date pudding recipe. I remember the years when you girls and Patty used to eat Thanksgiving dinner here and eat my pumpkin pie and then an hour or so later, march—or perhaps waddle down the street and eat a second dinner at Helen's and then manage to find room for her scrumptious date pudding. I told her you were pining for it, so she wrote it out for me.

1 egg
¾ cup molasses
1 teaspoon baking soda
½ cup water
1 ½ cups flour
½ teaspoon salt
1/8 teaspoon nutmeg
½ teaspoon cinnamon
1/8 teaspoon ground cloves
¾ cup chopped pitted dates
¼ cup chopped walnuts
2 tablespoons melted shortening or salad oil

Beat egg; add molasses. Dissolve soda in water; add to egg mixture. Sift together 1 ¼ cups flour, salt and the spices; add. Dredge dates and nuts with remaining flour. Add fat or oil (she says she uses oil). Fill a greased pudding mold ¾ full and cover tightly. Steam 1 hour and 30 minutes. Unmold and serve hot with dessert sauce (to follow) or ice or whipped cream. To die for. Helen really is a spectacular cook.

SATIN DESSERT SAUCE

1 egg white
½ cup powdered sugar
1 egg yolk
½ cup whipping cream
1 teaspoon vanilla
Teensy Dash salt

Beat the egg white stiff. Gradually add sugar, beating constantly. Beat egg yolk separately and fold in. Whip cream and fold in with the vanilla and salt. This makes 1 ½ cups.

It's really worth the effort if you go to all the trouble to make date pudding, which one does only once or twice a year.

SHOO-FLY PIE

When I made this one of the times the Craig's were here to visit, your Dad broke into the song about Shoo-fly Pie and Apple Pan Dowdy. Silly song, but he does have a very nice voice. I think in his secret heart of hearts he'd like to be Bing Crosby. I do dearly miss the Craig family that used to was. Including Peppy.

1 ½ cup sifted flour
1 cup brown sugar
¼ cup shortening
1/8 teaspoon salt
½ teaspoon baking soda
½ cup hot water

½ cup molasses
2 unbaked pie shells

Mix flour, sugar, shortening and salt and make into crumbs. Dissolve soda in hot water and combine with molasses. Pour into pie shells and top with crumbs. Bake in hot oven at 450 degrees for 10 minutes and then reduce heat to 350 degrees and bake for 20-30 minutes longer or until firm.

APPLE PAN DOWDY

Yesterday, Kane and I went on quite a jaunt. Kane drove and we went to Anderson and did some shopping. Most of it of the window variety but did buy a few trinkets. Kane bought a dress. Since I already had mine for the year, I bought none. I allow myself one dress per year and although I'm behind for the last four years, I did purchase one at Fermen's last year. Don't think I should make up the lost time. I'm much too frugal for that frivolity. We ate a light lunch at a restaurant. All in all, we were out for several hours. We were exhausted but it felt very good to be out and about.

Today, I'm making Apple Pan Dowdy. Sounds like the song, I know, but nonetheless, it's very tasty. Wish I could send you some of this. You love my Apple Dumplings and it's much like that. I used my good friend Bisquick. Someone was very smart to come up with that. I can't send it but was thinking of you as I made it. Thought I'd write as it's in the oven.

4 tart apples
½ cup sugar

½ teaspoon cinnamon
2 tablespoon butter
1 recipe from Bisquick for biscuits

Peel and slice apples and arrange them in a well-greased baking pan. Sprinkle with sugar and cinnamon and dot with butter. Cover with biscuit dough, rolled to about ½ in. thickness. Cut several slices in the dough for steam to escape. Bake at 350 degrees for about 30 minutes. May be served with caramel sauce.

NASTY SURPRISE CARAMEL CUSTARD

Here's a dessert that will both thrill and fill your innards! It's ever so simple and scrumptious, too. Pay attention to the part about not letting the water boil too low. Once years ago, when the children were small, I got distracted when our puppy went missing. Everyone was so distressed that I went to help look and came back to a royal mess. The can had boiled dry and exploded and there were sugary-milky globs in places you wouldn't even think to look. After all that, the puppy wandered out from behind the couch yawning and stretching after her delicious nap. So set a timer or something so you don't forget. Or don't have a dog!

1 can Eagle Brand condensed milk
1 pint whipping cream

In a large pan, place the unopened can of condensed milk. Add enough water to just below the top of the can. Cook at a low boil for 3 to 4 hours. Be certain to keep your eyes on the level of water. Do not let the water level get below half the can. Remove from heat and let cool to the touch.

Beat whipping cream to soft peaks. Open can of milk and spoon out caramel mixture. Top with a dollop of whipped cream and enjoy!

OLD-FASHIONED APPLE DUMPLINGS

I had some of the Rebekkahs over last night and served them my famous old-fashioned apple dumplings and there were sighs all 'round. I must admit that I do make a mean apple dumpling, if I do say so myself, as shouldn't. Of course, I guess if they were really old-fashioned, one would use a regular biscuit recipe, but you know what friends I am with Bisquick.

You girls have always been fond of my apple dumplings so am sending you the recipe for posterity. It is hard to give a regular recipe, for it depends on the number you want, but let's say enough for four, which is the number I made yesterday.

4 tart apples
3 cups light brown sugar
¾ cup granulated sugar
3 cups (or a little more) of water.
2 teaspoons cinnamon
2 cups Bisquick
Large chunk of butter—about half a stick.
¾ cup milk.

Turn on 350-degree oven. Pare and core apples and cut into quarters. Mix the cinnamon and sugar together and roll each quarter in this mixture. Stir milk into Bisquick. Beat dough hard for 30 seconds to make it tighten up enough to handle. Turn dough onto well-floured, cloth-covered board. Pat, round it up and fold over 3 times. Roll out lightly with rolling pin ½ inch thick into a more or less square. With a sharp knife, cut the dough into 16 even squares. Put one piece of sugared apple on a square of dough and fold the dough up around the apple, pinching it at the top. Repeat till you have 16 little dumplings. Place them in a buttered, deep pan. You can sprinkle on some more cinnamon if you like.

Put the butter, brown sugar and water in a small saucepan over low heat till butter melts and pour over the dumplings. Bake till apples are tender, about 45 minutes more or less.

These are nice with either ice cream or whipped cream. I served the former to the Rebekahs and there was nary a whimper. Some were not such big eaters, so fortunately there was a bit left over, which I plan to polish off for dessert tonight.

FUDGY BROWNIES

As you know I am not personally o'er fond of chocolate. I know that's almost heresy, but there it is. But I can't say the same for the Democrat Club, as they are veritable chocolate fiends. When I bring these brownies to a meeting there is a universal Huzzah! as they fall as one upon these tasty morsels, which are a cross between fudge and cake.

5 tablespoons butter cut into pieces
6 ounces semi-sweet chocolate, chopped
2/3 cup sugar
Largish Dash salt

2 large eggs
1/3 cup flour
1 cup walnut pieces

Light a 325-degree oven. Line an 8 x 8-inch baking pan with buttered tinfoil. Put a bowl over simmering water (my version of a double boiler) and drop in the butter followed by the chocolate and heat, stirring once in a while till melted. Remove the bowl and whisk in sugar and salt followed by the eggs, which you whisk in one by one. Stir this till it's smooth and then gently stir in the flour. Fold in walnuts.

Pour into the pan and smooth with a rubber spatula, after which you allow the nearest child to lick it. The other one can lick the bowl. Bake the brownies for 30 minutes or maybe a minute or two more till the top looks dull and a knife inserted into the center comes out clean.

When the brownies are cool, peel away the foil and cut into 16 squares. Then stand back while the Mongol hordes descend.

APPLE FRITTERS

I've been trying since before I came home from your house to get me a corset. I've been to the Anderson Mall and to Wasson's and Penney's and they will always have them in "next week." Fermen's had Playtex girdles on sale for $2.00 off and went to see them, though I knew I could not wear them, and lo and behold, she had the very kind of corset I wanted. So, I bought one--$10.95. Hated to invest that much but it will likely do me as long as I may need one. It reduces my waistline some, but unfortunately it does the same for my hips, so I still look like a post, for I am straight up and down from my armpits to my

kneecaps. Maybe if I ate something fattening like apple fritters, I'd start to get a shape.

2 large apples
1 cup flour
1 tablespoon sugar
1 teaspoon cinnamon
½ teaspoon salt
2 well-beaten eggs
2/3 cup milk
Cooking oil to deep fry
Powdered sugar

Core and slice apples from top to bottom. Mix together flour, sugar,
cinnamon and salt. Combine milk and eggs and pour into dry ingredients, mixing thoroughly to form a batter. Dip apples into batter and
drop into hot oil and cook until lightly browned. Drain on paper towels and sift powdered sugar over fritters. Serve warm or cold.

APPLE WHEAT BETTY

My housekeeping, while at best, never my strong suit, is at
worst at present. I just don't seem to get to things these days.
I'll have to get busy soon, for I have Pinochle Club two weeks
from tomorrow night and the house has most of the accumulat-
ed winter dirt. Bill gets the sweeper out and uses it fairly regu-
larly, but otherwise not much doing and I'd be embarrassed for
the "girls with the grandma faces" to see it as is.

When things get in apple pie order, I'm going to make Apple
Wheat Betty instead of a pie to serve them. This couldn't be
easier to make, and everyone likes it.

4 full-size shredded wheat biscuits
4 apples
1 cup firmly packed brown sugar
1 teaspoon cinnamon
1 cup coarsely chopped walnuts
2 tablespoons butter
1 tablespoon lemon juice
½ cup water

Heat oven to 350 degrees. Crush shredded wheat biscuits (this is fun). Pare apples; core; slice. Combine sugar and cinnamon. Place alternate layers cereal, nuts and apples in a baking dish, sprinkling the apple layers with sugar mixture. Dot with butter. Mix juice and water and add. Cover and bake for about 50 minutes. Serve hot with custard sauce if you're ambitious—good ole' ice cream or whipped cream if you're not.

Maybe if the dessert is good enough, they'll develop myopia and not see the dust. Here's hoping.

CUSTARD SAUCE

Sometimes if I'm feeling particularly energetic or am tired of ice cream or whipped cream, I make this delicious sauce for nearly any dessert. Or even by itself.

3 tablespoons flour
½ cup sugar
Dash salt
2 eggs
2 cups milk
1 teaspoon vanilla

Mix flour, sugar and salt. Beat eggs slightly; add. Heat milk to almost boiling. Gradually add. Cook over hot water (double boiler style) stirring constantly till it thickens and coats the spoon. Add vanilla and chill. (2 cups).

You can make this into chocolate sauce by adding 1 square of melted unsweetened chocolate and 3 tablespoons sugar to flour mixture. I wouldn't, however, use chocolate with the Betty.

YUMMY BREAD PUDDING (DUTY)

Mama and all the women her age used to call this 'Duty' 'cause it was a duty not to waste things and this used up the stale bread. I was always so skinny that Mama made this a lot, even with bread that wasn't stale, just 'cause she knew I liked it and she wanted me to eat it to put some meat on my bones. It never worked—I was "up" to 96 pounds at the doctor's the other day.

4-6 slices bread
½ cup raisins (optional)
3 eggs
3 cup milk
½ cup sugar (I like brown best)
2 tsp vanilla
teensy Dash salt

Turn on medium oven (350 degrees). Tear the bread into hunks and put in bottom of a baking dish. Sprinkle with raisins if using. Beat together the eggs, milk, sugar, vanilla and salt. Pour this over the bread and bake for about 35 minutes.

This won't make you fat—at least it never worked for me, but it'll make you feel like your Grandmother loves you, which she does, ardently.

OATMEAL COOKIES WITH RAISINS N' NUTS

When I took care of you while your mother worked during the war, I used to send these in your school lunches and you only later confessed that, not liking them, you had pulled out all the raisins. If you still don't like 'em, save yourself the trouble and don't put any in to start.

½ cup butter
¾ cup packed brown sugar
1 egg
1 ½ teaspoon vanilla
Teeny Dash salt
1 ½ cups flour (can use whole wheat)
¾ teaspoon baking powder
¾ cup rolled oats
¾ cup chopped walnuts
¾ cup raisins (optional)

Turn on oven to 375 degrees. Cream together butter and sugar, then add egg, vanilla and salt. In another bowl, sift together flour and baking powder. Add rolled oats and stir. Combine all ingredients along with walnuts and raisins and blend well. If the batter seems too dry to work with, add about a tablespoon of water. Drop by tablespoons on greased cookie sheets and flatten a little. Bake for 10-12 minutes. Give one to each child with a kiss from 'Ganu.'

BLACK WALNUT COOKIES

When I was a girl, we would gather fallen walnuts in the fall. ('s why it's called fall). We would gather great piles of them and let the green part sort of dry a bit and when it had turned black, we'd remove the outer covering. It always stained our hands an ugly yellowish brown that looked like nicotine stain and wouldn't wash off. It was a mark of pride amongst our fellow hoarders. Eventually it wore off. In the meantime, we'd crack the walnuts and sometimes make these cookies. I don't know if the walnuts were black or English. I don't suppose it matters to the taste of the cookies.

2 cups brown sugar
4 eggs, beaten
½ cup sifted flour
½ teaspoon baking powder
½ teaspoon salt
1 cup chopped walnuts

Heat oven to 375-degrees. Combine sugar and eggs and mix well. Sift flour, baking powder and salt and add to first mixture. Stir in nuts. Drop by teaspoon on a greased cookie sheet and bake for about 12 minutes. Should make about 6 dozen cookies.

CANASTA HERMITS

If I should live so long, I may become a first class cook. Annie says she does not understand how anyone as indifferent to food as I should be a good cook but have always loved to feed people. I am also not so indifferent anymore. Thursday afternoon

I had Nelle, Lillian and Venita here for Canasta. Lillian and I got beat both games but of course they did not play fair. Had a lot of fun and caught up on all the latest gossip. I made these little Hermits, which they enjoyed with coffee afterward. And I enjoyed not a few, myself.

1 cup sugar
½ cup shortening
½ cup molasses
½ cup lukewarm water
3 cups sifted flour
1 teaspoon baking soda
1 teaspoon ground cloves
1 teaspoon cinnamon
½ teaspoon salt
1 egg
1 cup raisins or dates, chopped fine

Heat oven to 350-degrees. Cream sugar and shortening. Add molasses and water. Add flour sifted with soda spices and salt, beaten egg and fruit. Blend well. Drop by teaspoons onto greased cookie sheet. Bake for 10-12 minutes. Should make about 70.

DUNKIN' SUGAR COOKIES

I am supposed to go up and get my store teeth tomorrow. I got them about Thanksgiving but have never been able to eat with them, so Kane and I went up last Saturday and I had them lined but had to leave them. I surely hope I have better luck with them now, for I am wasting away to a mere shadow of my former fat self. That was when I weighed nearly 97 pounds. I look pretty awful and dread having the children see me, for I fear they will do like the lass in Locksley Hall: "The maid turned slowly round—looked at me once and fell upon the ground."

When I was little Mama was always trying to fatten me up. She often made these cookies, 'cause I liked them so.

1 cup butter
½ cup sugar
1 egg
1 teaspoon vanilla extract
2 ¼ cups flour
1 ½ teaspoons baking powder
¾ teaspoon salt
Milk for brushing
Sugar for sprinkling

Heat oven to 400 degrees. Cream together butter and sugar. Beat egg and add along with vanilla. Sift together flour, baking powder and salt and add to wet mixture. Shape into 2 rolls, 2 inches in diameter; wrap in waxed paper. Chill until firm. Slice 1/8 inch thick. Place on greased baking sheet, brush with milk and sprinkle with sugar. Bake about 6 minutes.

If I made these now, I'd have to dunk them in my coffee, which Emily Post frowns upon, but she probably has all her teeth.

MY FAVORITE BIRTHDAY CAKE

May 12, 1964

My Dearies:

Knowing fate for the flirtatious vixen she is, I planned ahead for how I would celebrate my 80th birthday. I thought I should do something daring and outrageous but had a hard time coming up with anything, as I have already been up in an airplane and I've tasted hard liquor and couldn't think what else was left. I finally hit on the idea of smoking a cigarette.

My plans were thwarted, however, on several fronts. I thought I might buy a pack, but then couldn't think what I'd do with the other 19 cigarettes in the pack. To leave them unsmoked would be wasteful and I'd only planned on using just the one. I didn't want to smoke them all for fear of becoming a cigarette fiend. Then I thought perhaps I'd borrow one from your mother, but she would've known what I was up to and I was bashful about anyone else knowing. For the briefest period I considered slipping one out of her pack when she wasn't looking but stooping to theft was a bit more daring and outrageous than I felt myself capable of.

In the end, I did nothing scandalous but allowed myself to be feted instead with a birthday cake. Maybe I'll skydive for my 85th. Katie made my favorite Lady Baltimore Cake, which I include for your baking pleasure, should you be so inclined.

Cake:
¾ cup shortening
1 ½ cup sugar
3 cups cake flour

4 teaspoons baking powder
½ teaspoons salt
1 cup milk
1 teaspoon almond extract
5 egg whites

Set the oven to 375. Cream together shortening and sugar. Sift together flour, baking powder and salt and add alternately with milk
and almond extract to the creamed mixture. Beat the egg whites stiff
and fold in. Pour into 9" layer pans and bake 30 minutes. Cool 5
minutes and remove layers from pans. Cool on wire rack while you
make the icing.

Icing:
1 ½ cup sugar
½ cup water
1 ½ teaspoons white vinegar
3 egg whites
Teeny Dash salt
1 teaspoon vanilla extract
¾ cup toasted coconut

Boil the sugar, water and vinegar together till the syrup forms a long
thread when dropped from the tip of a spoon. Beat egg whites stiff
and gradually add the syrup, beating constantly until the icing hold
shape. Add salt and vanilla and fold in ½ cup of coconut. Ice the
cooled cake and sprinkle the remaining coconut on top.

This made me feel regal indeed and should be served to everyone on the occasion of their 80th birthday if they don't plan to
go deep sea diving, which I hadn't considered until just this
moment. Not that we have any deep sea around here.

MABEL'S OATMEAL CAKE

My appetite is capricious these days. I've been back on half and half with my coffee. For some reason or other cannot bear CoffeeMate just now. Same way with custard pie, and you know how fond I have always been of that. Mabel sent me one about every other day while Bill was in the hospital. I wanted anything then but food, and I just plain got fed up on them. I had one from someone else and gave it to Kane and no sooner did she pick it up than Mabel called and said, "Bob is on his way down with a custard pie." I took it very graciously but had a notion to tell her I would rather have had one of her oatmeal cakes. They are out of this world. Here is her recipe that I finally talked her out of.

Cake:

1 cup rolled oats
1 ¼ cup boiling water
1 cup white sugar
1 cup packed brown sugar
½ cup shortening
2 eggs
1 ½ cups all-purpose flour
1 teaspoon baking soda
½ teaspoon salt
½ teaspoon ground nutmeg

Icing
1 tablespoon melted butter
½ cup packed brown sugar
2 tablespoons heavy cream
2/3 cup flaked coconut
½ teaspoon vanilla extract

In a small bowl, stir oats into boiling water. Set aside to soak for 20 minutes.

Preheat the oven to 350 degrees. Grease an 8x8 inch baking pan.

In a medium bowl, cream together the white sugar, 1 cup brown sugar and shortening until smooth. Beat in the eggs one at a time. Sift in the flour, baking soda, salt and nutmeg; stir just until moistened. Mix in the soaked oats. Pour into the prepared pan and spread evenly. Bake for 35 to 40 minutes in the preheated oven, until a toothpick inserted into the cake comes out clean.

Turn the oven to the broil setting and let it heat up. In a small bowl, stir together the melted butter, 1/2 cup brown sugar, heavy cream, coconut and vanilla. Spread over the top of the cake. Broil for a few minutes, just until the coconut is lightly browned.

CHOCOLATE BUTTERMILK APPLESAUCE CAKE

I was perusing a magazine that Kane brought over the other day. Can't think which one it might have been. Maybe Good Housekeeping or Woman's Day or one of those. This recipe caught my eye and I decided to make it, as Harry and Trevella were coming over for supper and I needed something for dessert. I was "juberous" about the applesauce, as it did not seem to fit. Juberous was Mama's word, which does not appear in anyone's dictionary. I have come to decide from the way it was used that she meant dubious. However, the cake was moist and delicious, and all declared it to be a fine concoction, indeed. Here it is if you wish to try it.

3 ounces unsweetened chocolate
1 cup water
¾ cup sugar
1/3 cup cooking oil
1/3 cup unsweetened applesauce
1 large egg
1 teaspoon vanilla
½ cup buttermilk
1 teaspoon baking soda
1 ¼ cup flour
½ cup unsweetened cocoa powder
Dash of salt

Heat oven to 350. Butter an 8 x 8 baking pan. Melt chocolate into water in a small pan over medium-low heat and cool to lukewarm. Add sugar, oil, applesauce, egg, and vanilla and whisk until it's smooth. Mix the buttermilk and baking soda together in a cup. Now whisk the flour, cocoa and salt in a large bowl until thoroughly blended. Whisk in the chocolate mixture and the buttermilk.

Pour the batter into the pan and bake 35 minutes or until a toothpick or a spaghetti strand inserted in the middle comes out clean. I used to know a woman who used broom straws to do this, but I did think that after she'd swept her floor with it, it would be none too sanitary, so eschew the practice myself. Set the cake on racks until cool enough to ice.

CHOCOLATE COFFEE ICING

You could leave that cake un-iced, but this is very good on the cake.

1 teaspoon instant coffee
1 tablespoon hot water
1 stick butter (not oleo)
2 teaspoon unsweetened cocoa powder
1 ½ cup powdered sugar
1 teaspoon vanilla

Dissolve the coffee in the hot water in a bowl. Add butter, softened to room temperature, cocoa, sugar and vanilla and beat with an electric mixer. Spread on the cooled cake. And let the kids fight over the bowl and mixers. Well, I don't want my little angels to fight, so allot the bowl to one and the mixers to the other.

PEACH PIE

Betty and Carl came by the other day and brought me some homegrown peaches. So, there was nothing for it but to make a pie. I gave a big hunk to my neighbor, but with Bill gone, I'm hard pressed to finish the rest. Wish you were here to eat it with me.

1 cup sugar
2 tablespoons quick-cooking tapioca
Teensy Dash salt
1 teaspoon lemon juice
4 cups sliced peaches

2 tablespoons butter
Piecrust for 2-crust pie

Heat oven to 425. Mix sugar, tapioca, salt and lemon juice; combine with peaches and let stand 15 minutes or while you make the pie crust. Pour peach mixture into pie crust and dot with butter. Place top crust on and slit holes for steam. Bake 40 to 50 minutes.

MARY ANN'S SUGAR PIE

September 16, 1967

Today Mama would have been 129 years old and my guess is that she would still have been a doughty, dominant character. She lived alone for a while after Papa died, but then she moved in with us when your mother was a baby. She adored her little Jeanie. Mama had the most fearsome sweet tooth. While she could still do it, she would make this pie, which she loved. Later I would make it for her, to her delight.

¾ cup sugar
½ cup heavy cream
¾ cup brown sugar
2 egg yolks, beaten
2 tablespoons butter
½ teaspoon vanilla
Teensy Dash salt
2 egg whites
Nutmeg
Pie shell (recipe below)

Heat oven to 425 degrees. Cook sugar, cream, brown sugar, egg yolks and butter in a double boiler until it becomes thick. Make sure you stir constantly. Remove from heat, add vanilla, salt and beaten egg whites. Pour into unbaked pie shell, sprinkle with nutmeg and bake about 10 minutes. Reduce oven to 300 degrees and bake for about 45 minutes longer or until you can put in a knife and it comes out clean. I like to serve it cold.

PIECRUST

Here's the piecrust I make for all my pies. I hear tell you can buy piecrust already made, but surely it's an abomination. If I didn't feel like making a pie crust, I'd just make a crisp or something else civilized.

2 ½ cups flour
1/3 cup ice water (about)
1 teaspoon salt
¼ cup shortening

We used to use lard for the shortening, and it made the best pies, but these days I use Crisco. I suppose you could use butter. If you do, leave out the salt unless you use unsalted butter. Sift together the flour and salt. Use a pastry blender (or a couple of knives if you don't have one) and cut in the shortening till it's the size of peas. Add gradually just enough water to hold the ingredients together, sprinkling evenly and mixing with a fork to form a ball. Don't mess with it too much—makes it tough.

At this point you can wrap it tightly in wax paper and put it in the icebox while you make the pie filling. Then roll out half the dough in a circle about 1/8-inch thick on a floured board. Put one circle in the pie pan. If you're going to fill it with an unbaked filling, cut the excess off around the pan with a knife and crimp the edges; prick a few places with a fork and bake in a pre-heated 450-degree oven for 15 minutes. If you cut a largish piece of tin foil, fill it with a cup of beans and place it over the bottom of the crust, it won't blister as it bakes.

If you're making a two-crust pie, fill the lower half with pie filling and moisten the edge of the crust with water. Then fit the second half over the pie; cut off excess and pinch the edges to make a fluted rim. Cut slits in the center for the steam to escape. Follow directions for baking whichever pie

CHERRY CREAM PIE

October 22, 1965

Dear One,

I like to think I had an improper proposal on the bus on my way home from California, but I probably overestimate my charm. I sat with a very nice-looking young man whom I assumed to be in his middle seventies. He asked me if I had seen the Grand Canyon and I hadn't, and he asked me to stop off in Flagstaff with him and go out the next day. He even urged me mildly. Perhaps his intentions were entirely innocent, but I sort of like to think not. Nevertheless, I declined.

Back in the days before Perry and I were courting, I made this pie for an earlier beau. He said he'd marry me if I'd make it every day, but I didn't like to be loved for pie. Besides he was a bit *of a toper and his personal hygiene was not what it might have been. I think I must've had a cold when we first stepped out.*

1 graham cracker piecrust
1 tablespoon unflavored gelatin
½ cup cold water
2 cup canned sour cherries, drained
½ cup sugar
¾ cup cherry juice
Teensy Dash Salt
1 tablespoon lemon juice
½ cup whipped heavy cream

Prepare piecrust. Soak gelatin in cold water about 5 minutes. Heat cherries with sugar and juice. Add salt and softened gelatin. Mix well to dissolve gelatin. Add lemon juice and chill. When it begins to thicken, fold in whipped cream. Pour into piecrust. Chill in refrigerator at least an hour or until firm enough to cut.

GRAHAM CRACKER PIECRUST

6 Whole graham crackers
2 tablespoons butter

Crush graham crackers finely. Mix the crushed crackers with butter that is somewhat softened. Add a dollop of water and mix together until it all sticks together. Grease a 9-inch pie pan and press mixture in it to make a pie crust. Press it most of the way up the sides of the pan. Put into oven at 350 degrees for about 10 minutes. Let it cool before you fill it.

BAKED CARAMEL CORN

Don't be surprised if you hear of my demise. There is something virulent going around here and I just might catch it. There have been 11 deaths here in town in less than two weeks— some quite prominent. We will not profit from this bonanza, as Bill is no longer digging graves.

It will soon be Halloween and think I'll make popcorn balls to distribute to the various and sundry ghosts and goblins that will visit. They were quite popular last year.

2 cup light brown sugar
½ cup light corn syrup
2 sticks butter
½ teaspoon baking soda
Dash cream of tartar
Dash of salt
8 quarts popped corn

Mix sugar, corn syrup and butter in a heavy pan and bring to a boil. Cover the pan and turn the heat down slightly. Boil for 5 minutes. Remove from heat; add soda, cream of tarter and salt and immediately pour over popped corn. Mix lightly but thoroughly. Place in a large roaster pan and bake at 200 degrees for one hour. Pour out on waxed paper and separate pieces to cool. Or you could, while it's still warm, form it into balls. If you like, you can substitute two or three cups of nuts—pecans perhaps—for an equal volume of popcorn.

THANKSGIVING & CHRISTMAS DINNER

THE TURKEY

December 26, 1965

My Dear,

If I were a crying female I would have been submerged before noon yesterday. Your mother came and picked up Bill and me, and Harry's family drove separately, and all converged at your mother's where she had baked a 21-pound turkey. It was brown and beautiful and done to a turn. She had dressing, mashed and sweet potatoes, brown gravy and a pumpkin pie. Everything was very tasty, and we did full justice, but I swallowed a lump with each bite thinking of us all together last year. This year, Jean and I are back here in Indiana and Sue and family linger in California, whilst you and yours are off in the wilds of far Australia. 'Tain't right.

Now I'm going to pull myself together and tell you how to make the turkey your mother made. I have always made dressing outside the turkey, so this will be sans dressing.

18-20-pound turkey   1 stick melted butter
1 ¾ or more cup chicken stock (canned okay)
Poultry seasoning
¼ or ½ cup flour
Salt & pepper to taste

Remove the package of giblets and the neck from the turkey cavity. Put these into a medium size saucepan covered with stock and turn the heat on low. Remember to check on it from time to time, as it could boil dry. If it gets low, add more stock.

Then rinse the turkey with cold water inside and out and pat it dry with a towel or paper towels, if you have same. Tie the ends of the legs together and place the turkey, breast-side up on a rack in your turkey roasting pan. Brush melted butter over the turkey and sprinkle with poultry seasoning.

Roast at 325 for 4 to 4 ½ hours, basting occasionally with stock and/or butter. It is done when all is nicely browned, and the drumstick moves easily. If you happen to have a meat thermometer—I do now but roasted many a turkey without it—insert it into the thickest part of the meat making sure it doesn't touch a bone, which will throw the reading off. It should read 180 degrees.

Take it out of the oven, remove it to a cutting board with grooves to catch the juice and let it stand while you pour off as much as you can of the fat in the roasting pan. (I know. All that lovely butter!) Stir in the flour and place over medium heat on the stove. Be sure to scrape up all the brown nummies from the bottom of the pan. Gradually add the stock in which you've cooked the neck and giblets, stirring the while until it boils and thickens. If, by this time, some juice has accrued in the grooves of the cutting board, get someone to lift the turkey while you add said juice to the gravy. Salt and pepper to taste.

Get the man of the family to carve the turkey. It makes them feel necessary. Besides they need the exercise after watching all that football. Then everyone sit and though it be but ice water, raise your glasses to absent loved ones while you enjoy the Christmas repast.

CHESTNUT DRESSING
(Nearly as good as Mama's)

We used to love Mama's chestnut stuffing. I could never make it quite as good but it's pretty good, nonetheless. Chestnuts are pretty hard to come by these days. Not as popular as it used to be, I suppose. Too bad, because we used to get them frequently from our neighbors down the road in Carroll County, where I was raised. I'll try to tell you the recipe, but the chestnut gathering is on you. A bit of trouble but worth it.

1 lb. chestnuts
2 tablespoons cooking oil (I use Crisco)
¼ cup melted butter
¼ cup chicken broth
2 cups chopped celery
¼ to ½ cup chopped onion
1 tablespoon chopped parsley
6 cups breadcrumbs
1 egg beaten
Salt and pepper to taste

Put chestnuts into a pan of cold water and pick out the ones that float. Drain and dry and cut a ¼ - ½ in slit on both sides of nuts. Put into a pan and add oil. Cook over medium heat for about 5 minutes shaking pan while cooking. Place into oven at 450 degrees for another 5 minutes. When cool enough, using a paring knife, remove shells and brown skin.

Cover blanched nuts with salted water and simmer for about 20 minutes or until tender. Drain and mash. Combine chicken broth, butter, celery and onion and cook until tender. Remove from heat to add egg, parsley, breadcrumbs and chestnuts. Mix together and heat adding salt and pepper. Stuff chicken or turkey if that's what you do, while the stuffing is still warm. Should be enough for a 10/12 lb. turkey. Very tasty, indeed! As I've taken to making my stuffing separate from the turkey these days, one can do that too, but add a bit more liquid in the dressing for baking in the oven. I cover it and bake at 350 degrees for about 45 minutes and then uncover it for about 20 minutes.

ORANGE CANDIED SWEET POTATOES

Here is more or less, the way your mother fixed the sweet potatoes. I only lately added the orange juice, which I believe adds a tang that cuts through some of the sweetness.

3 or 4 largish sweet potatoes
Water for cooking
1 cup orange juice
¼ cup maple syrup
1 teaspoon ground ginger
1 ½ teaspoon cinnamon
1 ¼ teaspoon cardamom
1 ½ teaspoon salt
Bit of black pepper

Heat oven to 350. Peel and dice the potatoes and simmer in water for 5 minutes. Meanwhile, stir the remaining ingredients together. Spread them out onto a shallow baking pan. Drain the potatoes and scatter over the pan. Bake for 1 hour, stirring every-once-in-a-while until the potatoes are tender and well-coated with the resultant goo. Scoop all into a serving dish and modestly accept the kudos.

PERRY'S MINCE MEAT PIE

I had an enormous loin pork roast yesterday and your mother came but she ate only a small portion. I like to see a little more meat on her than she presently carries, but she may have my skinny heritage to contend with. At any rate, I was wondering what to do with the leftover pork when it dawned on me that I could make mincemeat. So, I hied me off to the kitchen and did so. Your granddad did dearly love his mincemeat pie. He could never resist a newly made pie. Sometimes if I was making it for company, I'd tell him if he cut into it early, I'd leave him. He always did and, thankfully I never did, though at the time I was sorely tempted. If you make this, it will remind you of him when you eat it.

3 cup apples, peeled and finely chopped
1 teaspoon cinnamon
¼ cup finely minced roast pork
½ teaspoon ground cloves
¾ cup brown sugar
1 teaspoon grated orange peel
1/3 cup seedless raisins
½ cup apple juice or cider
1 tablespoon vinegar
1 teaspoon salt
Sm. Amount of rum flavoring (if desired)

Heat all ingredients, except rum flavoring, to boiling point. Stir a few times while cooking. Reduce heat and simmer for 25 minutes. Stir in rum flavoring. Heat oven to 425 degrees. Roll out pastry for bottom crust. Place in pie pan and fill with mincemeat; cover with top crust. A lace crust made from strips looks very nice but I don't bother with it. Bake 30 minutes or until light brown. Serve with the usual whipped cream or ice cream topping, if desired. Because of the meat in the filling, keep in the ice box.

PUMPKIN PIE

I always make this for both Thanksgiving and Christmas and have never heard a complaint. Better double this and make two.

1 (15 ounce) can pumpkin
1 can Eagle Brand condensed milk
1 ¾ teaspoon pumpkin pie spice
½ teaspoon salt
2 eggs
1 unbaked piecrust

Heat oven to 425. Beat eggs in a large bowl and add remaining ingredients. Pour into the pie shell. Set the timer and bake for 15 minutes. Turn the oven down to 350 and bake for another 40 to 50 minutes. Test with a spaghetti strand in the center. When it comes out clean, cool on a wire rack.

The reason I always made at least two of these was that this was another pie your granddad couldn't resist cutting into ahead of time. That way I at least had one to present for company.

APPENDIX

GLOSSARY:
Grandmother terms:

Abashed: Dismayed, disconcerted, embarrassed.

Birch Bayh: Former Indiana senator

Canasta: A card game, a variety of Rummy.

Coxey's Army: In 1894 Jacob Sechler Coxey, a political reformer let a group of marchers (Coxey's Army) to Washington to petition Congress for legislation to relieve unemployment.

Denizens: Frequenters of a place

Doughty: Spirited, feisty, hardy, brave

Elucidate: To explain or make clear

Emily Post: Wrote a book and later a syndicated newspaper column on etiquette and good manners.

Epizootic: A disease that affects animals once thought to infect humans (may have been the flu).

Eschew: Avoid. Have nothing to do with.

Expedient: Means, method, device.

Geritol: A patent medicine marketed to an older population that promised pep and energy but delivered it in the form of a certain amount of alcohol in the liquid form.

Glaikit: An old Scottish word meaning flighty. She used it to mean 'walking around with your feet off the ground, head in the clouds.' She usually meant Jeanne Anne.

H & H: The sandwich shop and local teen hangout Harry owned and operated in Alexandria in the 50's.

Hied (me off): To hasten away, move with a degree of speed.

Homer Capeheart: Former Indiana senator

Hoosier Hysteria : The state of excitement surrounding the Indiana high school basketball tournaments.

Icebox: Refrigerator

Inveigle: Entice, influence, convince.

"Juberous": Grandmother thought this meant dubious from the way her mother used it.

Locksley Hall: A poem written by British Poet Laureate Alfred Lord Tennyson in 1835.

'Lowed: Allowed: Admitted, acknowledged.

Mr. Ed: A 60's TV sitcom about a talking horse.

Mr. Micawber: A character in "David Copperfield" by Charles Dickens. He was poor and had many children to feed. He never lost his optimistic belief that "Something would turn up" that would save them all from the poor house.

Munificent: Generous, bountiful

Myopia: Nearsightedness.

Nar-de-gar: Snooty, think they're better than others. (This is a term she used. We can't find it in the dictionary).

Nonplussed: Thrown, at a loss, mystified.

Onerous: Burdensome, tedious, time-consuming

Passel: Fairly large, indeterminate number.

Pinochle: a trick-taking game typically for two, three or four players and played with a 48 card deck. Popular in the Midwest.

Portliness: Beefiness, stoutness, corpulence. In other words, fatness.

Poultice: A soft, moist mass of cloth and/or herbs, applied to the body for medicinal purposes.

Progeny: Offspring, children, descendants

Provender: Provisions, food, grub

Purloining: Stealing

Rebekahs: The auxiliary group of the Odd Fellows Lodge, which were the first fraternal order in America to create a degree and a lodge for women

Stella Dallas: A tear-jerker radio soap opera that aired in the 30's and 40's.

Taciturn: Silent, quiet, reserved.

Toper: A hard drinker or chronic drunkard.

Ubiquitous: Ever present. You can find it everywhere.

Virulent: Dangerous, active, strong

Cooking terms:

Dash (of salt): Less than 1/8 teaspoon

Dredge: Sprinkle food with a powdered substance, usually flour or corn meal.

Glop: A generous serving placed (gently) on a plate.

Knob (of butter or other hardened fat). About 2 Tablespoons

Oleo: Margarine

Toast "soldiers": Slice buttered toast into 4 equal strips. Good for dipping into cocoa or a soft-boiled egg.

CAST OF CHARACTERS

Grandmother referred to a number of local people in her letters. For the curious here is a list of who they are. Nearly all residents of Alexandria, Indiana.

The author **Mary Goldie Montgomery Jolliff**, called variously **Goldie**, by some friends and many older family members, **Mary** by our grandfather and father, **Mary G,** by others, and **Jolliff** by the members of the Pinochle Club. And by her grandchildren: **Grandmother**. Always Grandmother, not Grandma. She said she was never a Ma and she's not a Grandma.

Perry, Our grandfather. We called him Granddaddy.

Jean, our mother who was divorced from our father during this period and lived in Marion, some 20 miles away.

Bill, Mother's ne-er-do-well brother who lived with Grandmother off and on during the period of the book.

Jack, another brother who married and moved to California during this period and his wife, **Norma**.

Harry, Mother's youngest brother who lived in Alexandria with his wife **Trevella** and their four children, **Lee, Graydon, Bruce** and **Lynn** and their smart dog, **Sam** until they moved to California in 1968.

Her cronies, neighbors and friends from Rebekahs and the Pinochle and Democrat Clubs: **Annie, Bertha, Kane, Mabel, Zelma, Mae, Katy, Nelle, Lillian, Venita, Mary.**

Hazel and **Edna,** Grandmother's nieces, daughters of her sister **Jenny.**

Carl, son of Aunt Jenny, and his wife **Betty.**

Rosemary, Uncle Bill's ex-wife, and **Adam**, the husband she married after the divorce.

Helen, our Mother's oldest friend, mother of **Patty,** our oldest friend, and her sisters **Mary Jo** and **June.**

Keri Jo, Craig and **Nikki**, Sue's children.

Sammy and **Alison** (AKA **Lance** and **Kat**), Jeanne Anne's children. Grandmother preferred the first names.

Ned, Grandmother's niece, daughter of her sister **Della**, and **Boyd**, Ned's husband.

Ethel, Grandmother's niece, daughter of her sister **Jenny**, and **Wayne,** Ethel's husband.

Billy Jim Gaither, of the Gaither Trio.

Frank, a painter in Alexandria who would hire Uncle Bill from time to time.

Peppy: The Craig dog.

Waller: Owner of Waller Transfer and the Point Tavern and our Uncle Jack's employer.

PORCH SWING POEMS

JONAH AND THE WHALE
By Mary Goldie Jolliff
Poet Laureate of Rebekah Lodge: Alexandria Chapter

Listen my dears and I'll tell you a tale,
A gruesome tale of a naughty whale.

This whale was ever a greedy fish,
Always looking about for a toothsome dish.

One night when all was dark and drear,
A man named Jonah drifted near.

"Aha," said the whale, this is some poor sinner
That the Lord sent here to be my dinner.

Poor Jonah went down in the maw of that whale
And his wildest efforts were of no avail.

He thrashed about from front to tail,
Praying, "Lord please help me get out of this whale.

The whale swam away but before very long,
He said to himself, "I think something's wrong."

"It looked quite tasty but now I see
That something I ate don't agree with me."

He paddled up to a sandy bar,
Thinking to rest for perhaps an hour

Then his gut gave a lurch and his tale gave a quiver
And out spewed Jonah in a stream like a river,

"Ah me," sighed the whale, his relief so complete
He at once made a vow that I herewith repeat:

"From this day henceforward no more will I treat
Everything that I see as something to eat.

I'll be more discerning and much more discreet
For the rest of my life I will not overeat."

Awash in virtue, the whale swam away
Sworn to change from the lesson that day

Thus, ends my tale, and ne'er for greed
Take more of aught than you really need.

THE JABBERWOCK
From "Through the Looking Glass
By Lewis Carroll

'Twas brillig, and the slithy toves
Did gyre and gimble in the wabe;
All mimsy were the borogoves,
And the mome raths outgrabe.

"Beware the Jabberwock, my son!
The jaws that bite, the claws that catch!
Beware the Jubjub bird, and shun
The frumious Bandersnatch!"

He took his vorpal sword in hand:
Long time the manxome foe he sought—
So rested he by the Tumtum tree,
And stood awhile in thought.

And as in uffish thought he stood,
The Jabberwock, with eyes of flame,
Came whiffling through the tulgey wood,
And burbled as it came!

One, two! One, two! and through and through
The vorpal blade went snicker-snack!
He left it dead, and with its head
He went galumphing back.

"And hast thou slain the Jabberwock?
Come to my arms, my beamish boy!
O frabjous day! Callooh! Callay!"
He chortled in his joy.

'Twas brillig, and the slithy toves
Did gyre and gimble in the wabe;
All mimsy were the borogoves,
And the mome raths outgrabe.

LITTLE ORPHANT ANNIE

James Whitcomb Riley (1849-1916)
INSCRIBED WITH ALL FAITH AND AFFECTION

To all the little children: -- The happy ones; and sad ones;
The sober and the silent ones; the boisterous and glad ones;
The good ones -- Yes, the good ones, too; and all the lovely bad
ones.

LITTLE Orphant Annie's come to our house to stay,
An' wash the cups an' saucers up, an' brush the crumbs away,
An' shoo the chickens off the porch, an' dust the hearth, an' sweep,
An' make the fire, an' bake the bread, an' earn her board-an'-keep;
An' all us other childern, when the supper-things is done,
We set around the kitchen fire an' has the mostest fun
A-list'nin' to the witch-tales 'at Annie tells about,
An' the Gobble-uns 'at gits you
Ef you
Don't
Watch
Out!

Wunst they wuz a little boy wouldn't say his prayers,--
An' when he went to bed at night, away up-stairs,
His Mammy heerd him holler, an' his Daddy heerd him bawl,
An' when they turn't the kivvers down, he wuzn't there at all!
An' they seeked him in the rafter-room, an' cubby-hole, an' press,

An' seeked him up the chimbly-flue, an' ever'-wheres, I guess;
But all they ever found wuz thist his pants an' roundabout:--
An' the Gobble-uns 'll git you
Ef you
Don't
Watch
Out!

An' one time a little girl 'ud allus laugh an' grin,
An' make fun of ever' one, an' all her blood-an'-kin;
An' wunst, when they was "company," an' ole folks wuz there,
She mocked 'em an' shocked 'em, an' said she didn't care!
An' thist as she kicked her heels, an' turn't to run an' hide,
They wuz two great big Black Things a-standin' by her side,
An' they snatched her through the ceilin' 'fore she knowed what
she's about!
An' the Gobble-uns 'll git you
Ef you
Don't
Watch
Out!

An' little Orphant Annie says, when the blaze is blue,
An' the lamp-wick sputters, an' the wind goes woo-oo!
An' you hear the crickets quit, an' the moon is gray,
An' the lightnin'-bugs in dew is all squenched away,--
You better mind yer parunts, an' yer teachurs fond an' dear,
An' churish them 'at loves you, an' dry the orphant's tear,
An' he'p the pore an' needy ones 'at clusters all about,
Er the Gobble-uns 'll git you
Ef you
Don't
Watch
Out!

PORCH SWING SONGS

POOR LITTLE JOE

VERSE 1
One day as I wandered, thru New York's gay throng
I met a poor boy who was singing a song
Although he was singing, he wanted for bread
And though he was smiling, he wished himself dead
CHORUS
Cold blew the blast and down came the snow
No place to shelter him, no where to go
No Mother to guide him, in the grave she lay low
Cast out on the cold street was poor little Joe
VERSE 2
A carriage passed by with a lady inside
She looked at poor Joe and she saw that he cried
He followed the carriage, she not even smiled
While fondly caressing her own darling child
VERSE 3
The lights are all out, and the clock has struck one
'Long came a policeman whose duties were done
He looked at poor Joe lying dead in the snow
Saying "God bless this poor boy whose name I don't know.

THE PARDON CAME TOO LATE.
Copyright, 1891, by Willis Woodward & Co.

A fair-haired boy in a foreign land at sunrise was to die;
in a prison-cell he sat alone, from his heart there came a sigh;
Deserted from the ranks, they said, the reason none could say;
They only knew the orders were that he should die next day;
And as the hours glided by, a messenger on wings did fly
To save this boy from such a fate-a pardon, but it came too late.

Chorus.
The volley was fired at sunrise, just after break of day,
And while the echoes lingered, a soul had passed away
Into the arms of his Maker, and there to hear his fate;
A tear, a sigh, a sad "good-bye "-the pardon came too late.

And 'round the camp-fire burning bright the story then was told;
How his mother on a dying-bed called for her son so bold;
He hastened to obey her wish, was captured on the way;
She never saw her boy so fair-he died at break of day;
And when the truth at last was known,
his Innocence at once was shown,
To save from such an unjust fate a pardon sent, but 'twas too late.

Chorus.

PLEASE DON'T SELL
MY DADDY NO MORE WINE
(Red Lane)
Â« Â© '69 Tree Publishing Â»

Please don't sell my daddy no more wine no more wine
Mama don't want him drinking all the time
Please don't sell my daddy no more wine no more wine
He may be no good but he's still mine
Late one night in Old Joe's friendly barroom
Two men were standin' drinking all alone
Thinkin' of the days they were younger
Talking about the women they had known
When there in the dim light of the tavern
A sweet young girl came softly to their side
And two one man surprised looked upon two tear stained eyes
And saw his own sweet daughter's there a crying
Please don't sell my daddy...
My daddy used to buy me pretty dresses
Now it's only hand-me-downs and worn out shoes
It's because of you I know that I wear these ragged clothes
For you're the man who sells my daddy booze
Her father looked down on the glass that he was holding
As the teardrops trickled down his solemn face
I been here Joe so long now it's time that I was gone
Going home to stay I'll never see this place
Please don't sell my daddy...
Don't you do it don't you do it
Don't you sell my daddy no more wine no more wine
He may be no good but he's still mine

Ed. Disclaimer: This song was published after the porch swing days,
but we believe that it would've been one of Grandmother's favorites

INDEX

CPSIA information can be obtained
at www.ICGtesting.com
Printed in the USA
FSHW011843260420
69602FS